Marine Air-Ground Task Force
Intelligence Dissemination

U.S. Marine Corps

DISTRIBUTION STATEMENT A:Approved for public release; distribution is unlimited

PCN 143 000150 00

MCCDC (C 42)
13 Jul 2004

E R R A T U M

to

MCWP 2-4

MARINE AIR-GROUND TASK FORCE INTELLIGENCE DISSEMINATION

1. Change the publication short title to read "MCWP 2-4" (vice MCRP 2-1C) and change PCN to 143 000150 00 (vice 144 000134 00).

PCN 143 000150 80

DEPARTMENT OF THE NAVY
Headquarters United States Marine Corps
Washington, DC 20380-1775

1 July 2003

FOREWORD

Marine Corps Doctrinal Publication 2, *Intelligence,* and Marine Corps Warfighting Publication 2-1, *Intelligence Operations*, provide doctrine and tactics, techniques, and procedures for intelligence operations. Marine Corps Warfighting Publication (MCWP) 2-4 *Marine Air-Ground Task Force Intelligence Dissemination*, complements and expands upon this information by detailing specific doctrine, tactics, techniques, and procedures for conducting intelligence dissemination in support of the Marine air-ground task force (MAGTF). The primary target audience of this publication is intelligence personnel responsible for planning and executing intelligence dissemination operations, as well as personnel who provide support to intelligence dissemination or who use results from intelligence operations.

MCWP 2-4 describes aspects of intelligence dissemination operations including doctrinal fundamentals, responsibilities, management, methodology and planning, and common forms of dissemination, such as estimates, studies, briefings, and reports. MCWP 2-4 provides the information needed by Marines to understand, plan, and execute intelligence dissemination operations in support of the MAGTF across the range of military operations.

Reviewed and approved this date.

BY DIRECTION OF THE COMMANDANT OF THE MARINE CORPS

EDWARD HANLON, JR.
Lieutenant General, U.S. Marine Corps
Commanding General
Marine Corps Combat Development Command

Publication Control Number: 144 000134 00

MARINE AIR-GROUND TASK FORCE INTELLIGENCE DISSEMINATION

TABLE OF CONTENTS

Chapter 3. Intelligence Dissemination Methodology

Chapter 4. Intelligence Dissemination Planning

Chapter 5. Intelligence Estimates and Studies

Chapter 6. Intelligence Briefings

Chapter 7. Intelligence Reports

Appendices

Figures

CHAPTER 1
INTELLIGENCE DISSEMINATION OVERVIEW

Intelligence dissemination is the delivery of intelligence to users in a suitable form. (Marine Corps Warfighting Publication [MCWP] 2-1, *MAGTF Intelligence Operations*) Successful Marine air-ground task force (MAGTF) intelligence dissemination reduces uncertainty and provides knowledge to battlefield decisionmakers when and where required. Dissemination management involves establishing dissemination priorities, selection of dissemination means, and monitoring the flow of intelligence throughout the command. (Marine Corps Reference Publication [MCRP] 5-12C, *Marine Corps Supplement to the Department of Defense Dictionary of Military and Associated Terms*)

Objective

Dissemination management involves dissemination priorities, selection of dissemination means, and monitoring the flow of intelligence throughout the command. The objective of dissemination management is to deliver the required intelligence to the appropriate user in the proper form at the right time, while ensuring that individual consumers and the dissemination system are not overloaded by attempting to move unneeded or irrelevant information. Dissemination management also provides for the use of security controls, which do not impede the timely delivery or subsequent use of intelligence, while protecting intelligence sources and methods. (MCRP 5-12C)

Communications and Information System Factors

The MAGTF must ensure that sufficient communications and information systems (CIS) connectiv-

ity, with supporting intelligence resources, are integrated throughout the MAGTF staff intelligence element (G-2/S-2), and within the MAGTF's command and control (C2) structure. All sources of intelligence pertinent to the MAGTF's assigned mission(s) must be identified, quickly retrieved, processed, tailored to the supported requirement, and made available to planners and decisionmakers at all MAGTF echelons in sufficient time to be of value in their operations.

The fielding of numerous operational and intelligence-related automated systems and the challenges of joint, combined, and multinational operations make MAGTF intelligence dissemination a complicated endeavor. The MAGTF CIS architecture must link production with supported commanders. In addition to transmitting imagery and other intelligence products with large data files, the dissemination requirement includes the capability to disseminate sensitive compartmented information (SCI), and general service (GENSER) reports digitally via fiber-optics, wire or radio formats; and the capability to disseminate intelligence in voice formats.

Key MAGTF CIS resources include the following:

- Tactical data network (TDN).
- Nonsecure Internet Protocol Router Network (NIPRNET).
- SECRET Internet Protocol Router Network (SIPRNET).
- Defense Switched Network (DSN).
- Defense Secure Network (DSNET).
- Joint Worldwide Intelligence Communications System (JWICS).
- Intelligence analysis system (IAS).
- Command and control personal computer (C2PC).
- Intelligence operations workstation (IOW).

- Joint deployable intelligence support system (JDISS).
- Satellite communications (SATCOM).

For detailed descriptions of MAGTF CIS, see MCWP 3-40.3, *Communications and Information Systems.*

Intelligence Dissemination Capabilities and Challenges

Dissemination Assets

The intelligence battalion collection management and dissemination section provides the core C2 for Marine Expeditionary Force (MEF) intelligence dissemination operations by developing and coordinating the dissemination plan and reporting criteria. The surveillance and reconnaissance cell (SARC) executes reporting criteria. The production and analysis (P&A) cell receives collected intelligence data and information, analyzes it, produces intelligence products, and executes dissemination criteria. Key CIS resources required include IAS and JDISS, with access to the full range of MAGTF communications (JWICS, SIPRNET, NIPRNET or DSN) for external dissemination; and IAS via the TDN and other MAGTF communications resources for internal dissemination.

Internal Dissemination

The IAS, the IOW, and MAGTF TDN are the key tools for electronic dissemination between the command element (CE) and major subordinate commands (MSCs). Communications connectivity between the MAGTF CE and its major subordinate element (MSE) headquarters are predominantly provided by SATCOM, supplemented where practical with high frequency/ultra high frequency (UHF) radios, troposcatter multichannel radio systems, telephone systems, and couriers. IAS will be available at all command echelons down to the maneuver bn/squadron levels.

External Dissemination

The MAGTF CE will attempt to exploit all available external capabilities (national, theater or joint) to satisfy its intelligence requirements (IRs). Intelligence agencies and Department of Defense (DOD) organizations have varying connectivity and procedural requirements. These may be planned for and coordinated through the joint staff intelligence element (J-2) and the joint CIS staff element (J-6) or the Marine Corps forces (MARFOR) headquarters (HQ).

Major Subordinate Command Level and Below

Connectivity at the MSC level and below is principally via the TDN, single-channel radio, multichannel radio, telephone, and courier. Communications connectivity below the regiment/group level depends on a combination of tactical data systems and single channel radio. The ability to exchange data traffic may be limited due to the availability of bandwidth.

Responsibilities

Meeting MAGTF intelligence dissemination requirements requires extensive planning, coordination, situational awareness, flexibility, and perseverance. The CIS officer's focus is on providing the necessary communication channels, interfaces, and media necessary to move intelligence throughout the MAGTF, and to lateral elements and higher echelons. The intelligence officer remains focused on the employment of allocated CIS resources that support intelligence dissemination requirements while maintaining close coordination with the operations officer to monitor current and future operational missions and requirements.

Intelligence officers at every level of the MAGTF have dissemination responsibilities. At the MEF level, the intelligence battalion directs intelligence dissemination operations. The intelligence battalion commander/intelligence support coordinator (ISC) has principal staff responsibility for the dissemination architecture. The intelligence battalion commander is dual-hatted as the ISC. The collection management/dissemination officer (CM/DO) plays a key role in ensuring intel dissemination.

The CM/DO is sourced from the intelligence battalion's S-3 section. The CM/DO is responsible for the following:

- Formulating detailed intelligence collection requirements (ICRs) and intelligence dissemination requirements (IDRs) and tasking and coordinating internal and external operations to satisfy these.
- Receiving validated priority intelligence requirements (PIRs) and IRs and direction from the ISC, and then planning and managing the best methods to employ organic and supporting collection and dissemination resources through the intelligence collection and dissemination plans.
- Validating and forwarding MEF and MSC requests for national and theater collection and dissemination support using appropriate intelligence tools and procedures.
- Coordinating intelligence-related CIS requirements and maintaining awareness of available CIS connectivity throughout the MAGTF and with key external organizations.

The CIS officer (G-6/S-6) is responsible for the management and functioning of MAGTF CIS circuits, such as MEF radio nets and SIPRNET connectivity. The G-2/S-2 is responsible for the management and maintenance of dedicated intelligence systems. Regardless of the status of CIS support, the intelligence officer is responsible for the timely dissemination of critical intelligence.

Dissemination Guidelines

Guidelines for intelligence dissemination include the following:

- Dissemination formats; either verbal, text or graphical.
- Whether verbal, text or graphic, intelligence products should use standard formats whenever possible to facilitate ease of preparation, usability, and dissemination.
- Transmission can be either hardcopy or electronic, regardless of the format.
- Dissemination of too few or too many intelligence products can adversely affect operations.
- Intelligence dissemination requires sound judgment when applying information management techniques.
- Effective intelligence dissemination requires that intelligence personnel be aware of enemy capabilities and probable courses of action (COAs), as well as friendly missions, the commander's intent, and the concepts of operations.
- Successful MAGTF intelligence dissemination requires planning, management, and flexibility.
- Executing intelligence dissemination requires knowledge of manual and automated dissemination means available to the MAGTF.

Intelligence Dissemination and Intelligence Functions

MAGTF intelligence dissemination must support the following six specific intelligence functions:

- Support to the commander's estimate.
- Situation development.
- Indications and warning (I&W).
- Support to force protection.
- Support to targeting.
- Support to combat assessment.

Intelligence Dissemination within the Intelligence Cycle

The process used to develop intelligence is called the intelligence cycle (see fig. 1-1). The intelligence cycle consists of six sequential yet interdependent steps: planning and direction; collection; processing and exploitation; production; dissemination; and utilization. While consistent with the joint intelligence cycle, the Marine Corps cycle emphasizes the importance of intelligence utilization. MAGTF intelligence dissemination must be planned for and supervised to the same degree as direction, collection, processing, and production to ensure that intelligence operations are successful.

Intelligence Dissemination Criteria

The following criteria determine how well disseminated intelligence contributes to tactical success:

- Pertinence.
- Usability of form.
- Timeliness.
- Security.

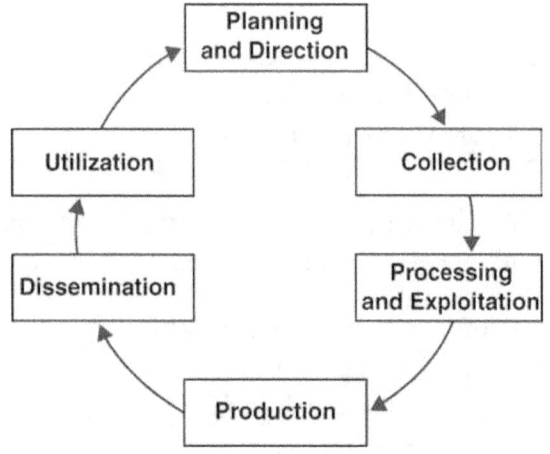

Figure 1-1. The Marine Corps Intelligence Cycle.

Pertinence

The dissemination system must provide the flexibility to use a supply-push system (which pushes important or time-sensitive intelligence directly to users), while also permitting users to demand-pull (allowing users to access information) relevant intelligence as needed from readily accessible sources, such as a database or a watch section at an intelligence center. The following principles guide successful dissemination of pertinent intelligence:

- *Relevant intelligence must be disseminated to all units or agencies that require it.* Intelligence must be tailored to the needs of the commander. Stated requirements are a minimum, and often change. Aggressive management of the dissemination strategy, a thorough understanding of user needs, sound judgment, and continuous monitoring of the dissemination architecture are required. Tactical judgment is important to disseminate pertinent intelligence to affected users, whether a requirement for it is a stated requirement or not.

- *Disseminate critical information and intelligence.* Disseminate intelligence, not simply information, to supported decisionmakers. However, because of its highly perishable or critical nature, combat data (derived from reporting by operational units) and sensor data may be disseminated without being converted into intelligence. Caution is required since warnings and combat and sensor data may later be explained in ways other than reflected in the original report. Additionally, this type of information has the potential to be over-disseminated. Operational rules of engagement must match the command's time-sensitive targeting policy.

- *Crisis situations may preclude some or all of the normal filtering process.* Filtering is a responsibility shared among intelligence collectors, producers, and disseminators, as well as among intelligence and other warfighting personnel. When time-sensitive crisis situations preclude deliberate intelligence processing and necessitate dissemination of untailored intelligence or unevaluated information, intelligence personnel must ensure that tactical commanders are aware that they are receiving unevaluated intelligence.

● *Dissemination downward should be selective and well planned.* Units should not receive irrelevant intelligence or voluminous amounts of information that can tie up their communication channels or overload their organic analytical capability. This is especially valid in the case of dissemination to lower tactical units whose capabilities for processing and producing information are limited. However, broad dissemination that results in the occasional delivery of intelligence to a non pertinent unit preferable to selective dissemination in which units may fail to receive available intelligence when they need it.

Usability of Form

Disseminated intelligence must be in a form suitable for immediate use by the recipient and should be tailored for the intended consumer. Standard formats for intelligence products—such as the intelligence estimate, intelligence studies, briefings, and reports—must be established, understood, and used by intelligence personnel and users. Basic MAGTF intelligence products have established formats. Individual units may modify formats if necessary, but modifications must be thoroughly coordinated as they may impact interoperability. Intelligence personnel should complement textual data with graphics when appropriate. Forms of dissemination include the following:

● *Written documents.* Intelligence estimates, operation plan/operation order (OPLAN/OPORD) annexes, studies, and reports are useful for general dissemination of large amounts of intelligence to many users—particularly within larger organizations when time is not critical and when deliberate planning is possible—and for all organizations in support of specified wartime contingency planning.

● *Messages.* Textual and voice messages may be effective for either routine or time-critical situations, particularly if restricted to a single intelligence subject, issue or action. It is important, however, that formats be standardized and understood by all—particularly if abbreviations or codes are used to aid with brevity.

● *Oral briefings.* Oral briefings, especially when built around a situation map and focused supporting graphics and imagery, are often used during deliberate and rapid planning and are the norm for intelligence dissemination to the immediate commander and his staff.

● *Electronic dissemination.* Automated technologies, including web-based technologies and information systems, are advancing opportunities for intelligence personnel at all command echelons to employ capabilities such as demand-pull, video-teleconferencing, and enhanced graphical techniques to access intelligence community resources.

Timeliness

Intelligence must be disseminated in time to influence planning, decisionmaking, and execution. Rapid dissemination of critical, time-sensitive intelligence is particularly vital. The commander's intent and the commander's critical intelligence requirements (CCIRs) guide the intelligence staff in identifying PIRs and anticipating future IRs. Many factors influence the timeliness of disseminated intelligence, including the following:

● Date desired is the date-time-group of when the requester requires the intelligence product and is a key dissemination planning factor.

● Latest time intelligence is of value (LTIOV) should be designated in cases where the value of intelligence collection would still be of use even if received after the specified date desired. LTIOVs should be written into PIRs for incorporation into dissemination operations planning and management.

- A high volume of intelligence reporting can degrade the performance of available intelligence communication networks and overwhelm scarce analytical resources.
- Distance, mobility, and terrain factors often limit available CIS options, such as automated wide-area networks (WANs), thereby increasing reliance upon less effective single channel radio and courier methods.
- The communications means available.
- The need to reformat certain intelligence products into user-friendly formats prior to dissemination.
- A heightened tempo that usually produces a greater quantity of IRs and customers.
- Hardware and software requirements that may pose interoperability or security problems, especially in joint or multinational operations.

The timeliness of intelligence dissemination may be improved by—

- Assigning priorities to intelligence requiring dissemination.
- Targeting specific recipients for each intelligence product.
- Reducing volume.
- Developing well-defined procedures.
- Training.

Security

Transmitting intelligence securely precludes the enemy from ascertaining MAGTF intelligence sources, estimating the effectiveness of MAGTF intelligence operations, and altering his actions or strengthening his counterintelligence (CI) efforts. Secure intelligence dissemination must be planned for and integrated with all command security programs: operations, information, communications, personnel, and physical security. Intelligence can be disseminated by any system available that provides adequate information security.

Secure dissemination methods must be used whenever possible. However, if the situation and intelligence are time-sensitive, intelligence may be disseminated via any available means. In such cases, the unit security manager and intelligence officer are immediately informed and will assess any possible damage and initiate necessary remedial corrective actions.

The majority of today's tactical CIS have integral or supporting features that provide security protection. For more restricted operational or SCI communications, detailed procedures exist that allow for sanitization and timely, broader dissemination when necessary. The principal security challenge that may be faced during tactical or crisis situations is when events occur that disrupt or degrade these unit CIS, necessitating a potential trade-off between security and dissemination. Multilateral operations raise additional dissemination challenges regarding the sharing of intelligence among allied and coalition forces.

Tailored intelligence will be disseminated via the best means available consistent with the operational situation. Although most intelligence will be classified, even some unclassified intelligence may require security protection due to operational security considerations. Resolving these challenges will be situationally dependent. Relevant factors to consider include the following:

- The enemy's own intelligence collection, processing, and dissemination capabilities.
- Phase of the operation's planning or execution.
- Significance of current intelligence gaps, particularly at lower tactical units.
- How the intelligence may support the exploitation of threat vulnerabilities and tactical opportunities.

Chapter 2
Intelligence Dissemination Management

Dissemination management ensures that the required intelligence is provided to the appropriate user in the proper form and at the right time.

Dissemination Management Functions

The two distinct functions within dissemination management are dissemination requirements management, and dissemination operations management. Dissemination requirements management defines what intelligence will be disseminated and who needs it; dissemination operations management specifies how the intelligence will be disseminated. Management of dissemination requirements and operations is performed at all levels of the MAGTF. Within

the MEF, management is coordinated by the intelligence battalion in accordance with the direction of the MEF intelligence officer.

Dissemination Requirements Management

Managing intelligence requirements is the first step in dissemination planning. Intelligence collection, production, and dissemination all flow from an integrated intelligence planning and direction process that is built upon IR management. Each IR will generally have an associated ICR, intelligence production requirement (IPR), and IDR. (See fig. 2-1) See also MCWP 2-1.

Dissemination requirements management is framed by the dissemination strategy, which incorporates commander's intent, CCIRs, PIRs, IRs,

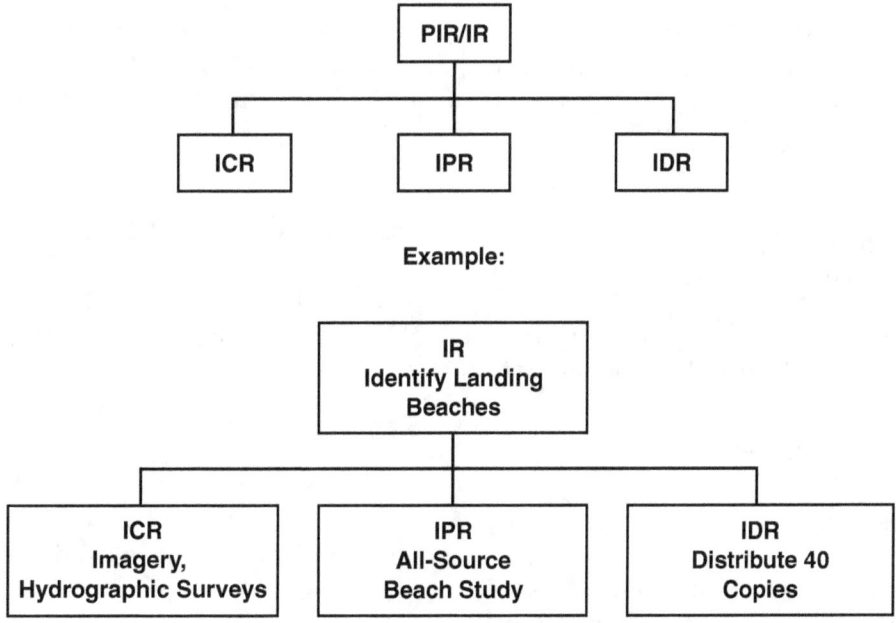

Figure 2-1. Requirements Satisfaction.

concepts of operation, and requests for information (RFIs). A preplanned dissemination strategy familiarizes the MAGTF with which intelligence products will be disseminated and by what means. It also describes alternate means of dissemination.

Dissemination Operations Management

Dissemination operations are managed by using a combination of methods (supply-push and demand-pull), channels (standard and alarm), modes (broadcast and point-to-point), and forms (verbal, text, and graphic) to convey the product to users.

Intelligence Dissemination Means

The ability to deliver tailored intelligence products and support to the right people in a timely manner is a direct result of the means of dissemination available. Within the MAGTF, no single way of disseminating will be satisfactory for all recipients and for all situations.

A combination of methods, channels, modes, and forms are planned, managed, and employed to accomplish the intelligence dissemination goal. These will vary according to the following:

- Situation.
- Location of the recipient.
- Urgency of the intelligence.
- Complexity or nature of the intelligence.
- Disseminating and receiving intelligence sections' capabilities.
- Available dissemination means.

Dissemination Methods

The two basic methods used to disseminate intelligence are supply-push and demand-pull. Intelligence planners must develop and implement intelligence dissemination plans with the flexibility to exploit either methodology, pushing time-sensitive intelligence directly to users while simultaneously allowing them to pull other intelligence products as needed.

The supply-push method disseminates intelligence to users as it becomes available (or on a schedule) from an intelligence collector or producer. This method is need-driven and is triggered by the availability of required intelligence and an understanding of its need by specific users.

The demand-pull method exploits technological improvements by giving users either direct electronic access to intelligence databases, files, servers or intelligence products through detailed search procedures or via direct queries to intelligence planners and producers, such as the MEF's P&A cell or the joint intelligence center (JIC).

Demand-pull dissemination is primarily used when there is a need by a subordinate command to access intelligence archives at higher HQ, such as databases and technical files maintained at JIC and the P&A cell for amplifying intelligence to support its planning activities (for example, basic/descriptive intelligence, technical information). It may also be employed by higher echelons to satisfy IRs when the amplifying data can best be accessed from subordinate units.

Dissemination Channels

Intelligence is disseminated using two types of channels: standard and alarm (see fig. 2-2).

Standard Channel

Standard channel dissemination consists of transmission of intelligence according to a set order and format. It is used for routine intelligence dissemination and is the channel used for the majority of dissemination requirements. Dissemination generally occurs on a regular schedule or intervals. Examples of standard intelligence dissemination include studies,

Standard Channels

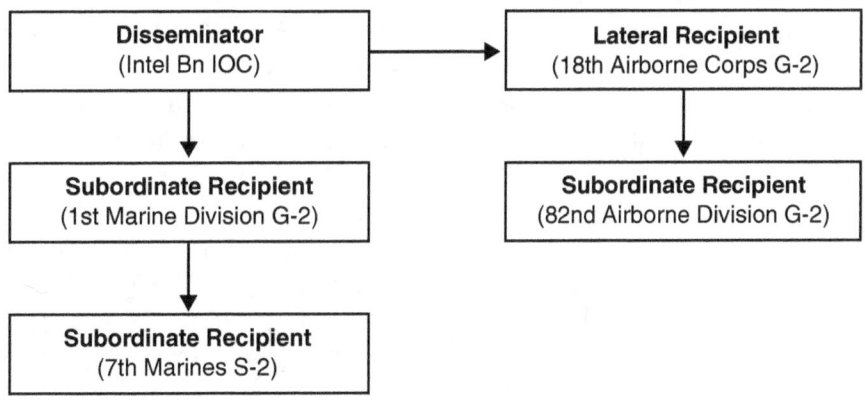

Alarm Channels

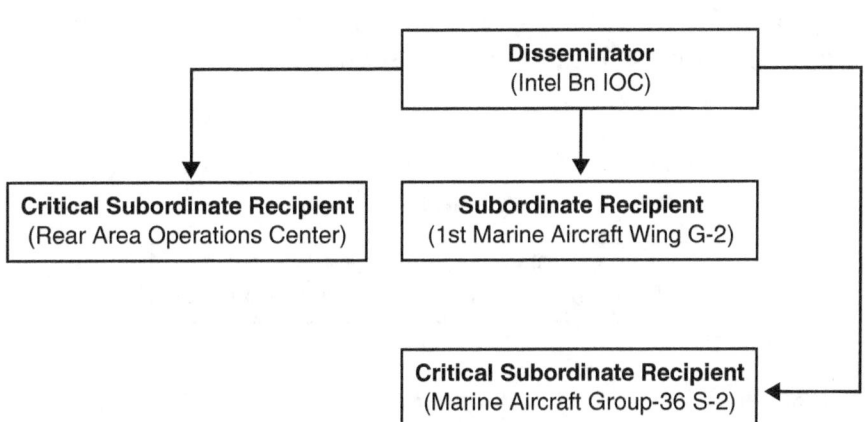

Figure 2-2. Intelligence Dissemination Channels.

reports, routine message intelligence summaries, and formal staff briefings. Standard dissemination employs normal MAGTF command and staff channels and supporting CIS.

Alarm Channel

Alarm channel dissemination is used for critical, time-sensitive intelligence that can have an immediate effect on operations. This type of dissemination has no set format or schedule and is activated only when critical intelligence is received that requires immediate decision or action. When an alarm-triggering event occurs,

intelligence must go to the units or sections most affected by the most direct means possible, even if it means skipping echelons of command. CIS connectivity may be either the standard MAGTF CIS architecture or by dedicated intelligence CIS. Because alarm intelligence is time-sensitive, dissemination should include a means for verifying receipt and understanding. Filters and thresholds for alarm-triggering events must be developed, understood, and practiced in advance. Effectively disseminating intelligence via alarm channels requires the following:

● Detailed intelligence collection, production, and reporting direction.

- Accurate knowledge of MAGTF CIS.
- Frequent interoperability training (to include other Service and joint organizations).
- Training for intelligence, operations and unit personnel to immediately recognize, act upon received intelligence, and disseminate it.

Dissemination Modes

Intelligence is disseminated via broadcast or point-to-point modes (see fig. 2-3).

Broadcast Mode

When using the broadcast mode, intelligence that affects the majority of units is disseminated simultaneously to a broad audience. Examples include dissemination of the initial MAGTF intelligence estimate or an I&W report of an enemy surface-to-surface missile launch. Successful use of broadcast modes depends on judicious selection of what intelligence is disseminated, the ability of all pertinent recipients to monitor the broadcast, and the ability of users to filter and select relevant intelligence for detailed examination. The broadcast mode improves dissemination timeliness, but must be used with discipline to avoid overloading MAGTF CIS pathways or intelligence processing capabilities.

Point-to-Point Mode

In the point-to-point mode, intelligence is disseminated to a specific user, normally in response

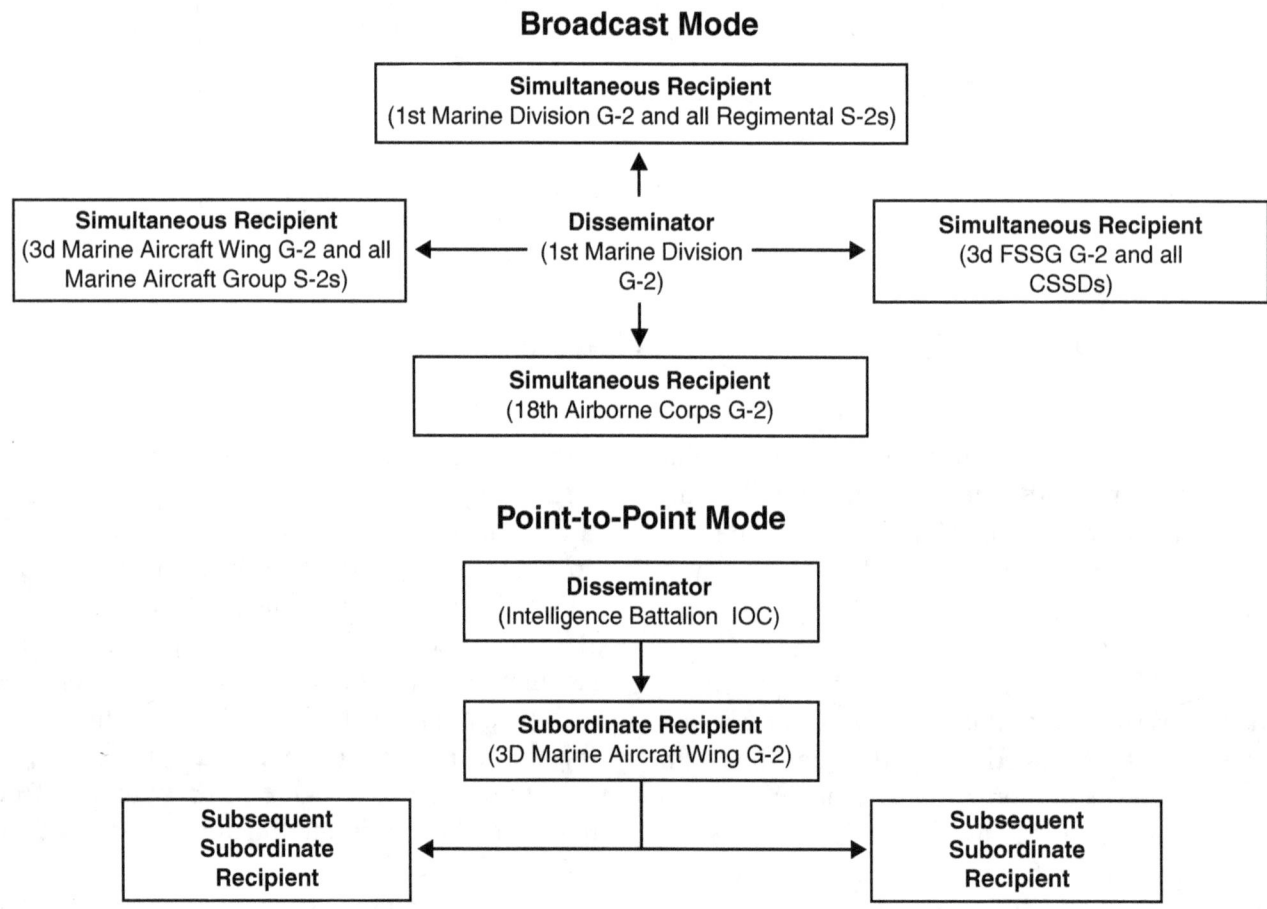

Figure 2-3. Intelligence Dissemination Modes.

to previously stated IRs. From there it may be further disseminated by users to others as appropriate. Although this mode is generally slower than the broadcast mode, it allows for intelligence to focus on specific user needs and allows the recipient to act as a control mechanism, filtering and integrating intelligence prior to disseminating it further. This control mechanism, however, adds risk as the intelligence meaning may become distorted as it is conveyed from one command to another. Examples of point-to-point modes include email, voice radio or telephone, and courier. When a secure WAN or local area network (LAN) is operational, a majority of intelligence disseminated between the MEF and its MSCs may be via email. Below the MSC level, the majority of point-to-point dissemination is by radio, wire communications or courier.

Dissemination Forms

The most suitable format for intelligence dissemination depends primarily on the needs of the recipient, the nature and urgency of the intelligence, and the means available to convey the information. The unit intelligence officer should specify a desired format (such as verbal, text, electronic) whenever stating an IPR and or/IDR.

Verbal

Verbal formats include dissemination via radio or telephone, face-to-face briefings, and discussions or via video-teleconferencing. The primary benefit of verbal formats is timeliness, in getting the information to the user, and by the disseminator having immediate, positive verification of delivery. Verbal forms can also enhance communication through subtle factors, such as tone of voice, inflection, facial expressions, body language, and gestures, which may convey greater meaning than the words alone. Verbal formats may be part of formal briefings that require complex graphics, detailed scripting, and rehearsals, which can monopolize personnel and material resources.

Text

Much intelligence is disseminated via documents, which may take many formats: plans, studies, analyses, estimates, assessments, reports, and electronic messages. Document dissemination provides a ready reference source, but may become obsolete, and may be difficult to rapidly and broadly disseminate during tactical operations.

Electronic

Many intelligence reports, databases, and sensor data are disseminated and updated electronically to improve timeliness and enable near real time connectivity between intelligence collectors, producers, and users. Examples include tactical LANs and WANs, and systems such as the JDISS and the IAS.

Reports

Intelligence reports and summaries are normally used to broadcast information electronically to a wide audience to update a current situation or subject of interest. Normally released according to a predetermined time schedule, reports continuously "refresh" databases but may lag in timeliness during a fast-moving crisis or battle.

Databases

Many intelligence-related databases are available for electronic dissemination. Threat and environmental databases are maintained within the intelligence battalion's P&A cell. Subordinate units establish and maintain their own databases, tailored to their units' intelligence needs.

Sensor Data and Information Streams

The G-2/S-2, G-3/S-3, and G-6/S-6 must coordinate sensor data and information management and dissemination-related issues, weigh the advantages and risks, and develop procedures. One example is the potential dissemination of intelligence information (for example, video footage) directly from a collector (for example, an unmanned aerial vehicle) to a targeting or operational node perhaps via an intelligence operations node.

Graphical Products

Graphics, such as those used in map enhancements or contained in annotated imagery, portray vast amounts of intelligence in a condensed form more easily interpreted by the human mind. When appropriate, they should be incorporated in intelligence production and dissemination. The chief benefit of graphical dissemination formats, such as maps, overlays, annotated imagery, briefing graphics, and topographic products, is that they may be assimilated and understood by people more quickly than textually-based formats. Effective use of graphical product dissemination requires standards, procedures, and training. In most cases intelligence disseminated via graphics must be reinforced with supporting documents or supplemental information.

CHAPTER 3
INTELLIGENCE DISSEMINATION METHODOLOGY

Dissemination planning begins with an understanding of basic dissemination methodology. The three parts of IR are ICR, IPR, and IDR. Each IDR should be processed individually, using the methodology described in figure 3-1.

Determine Dissemination Requirements

Identify what intelligence is needed, who needs it, location, date required, and assign priority. Disseminators should—

- Optimize utilization.
- Stay in contact with commanders and other intelligence requestors.

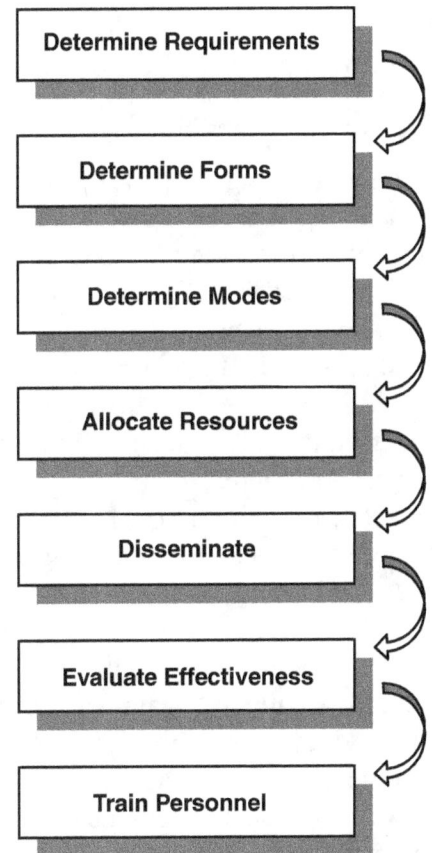

Figure 3-1. Dissemination Methodology.

- Determine common IRs.
- Develop planning tools.

Determine Dissemination Forms

Intelligence may be disseminated in a variety of formats and via verbal, text or graphical formats. The optimal form for dissemination best meets the needs of the user. It must answer the user's needs in the timeliest manner consistent with the urgency of the tactical situation.

A well-designed dissemination plan will take formatting factors into account and save man-hours otherwise spent on re-drafting and copying. Disseminators must be able to prepare and transmit the formatted intelligence in time to satisfy the user's LTIOVs. The format of the intelligence product must be compatible with the mode of transmission.

Dissemination planners must know the CIS capabilities and status of all supported elements. Since the CIS status of recipients may change at any time, disseminators must plan for alternate means of dissemination. Intended recipients in a highly mobile situation may be reliant on point-to-point phone or radio communications.

Determine Dissemination Modes

MAGTF intelligence staffs must identify dissemination channels and capabilities and plan for primary and alternate dissemination via common communication pathways. Available CIS bandwidth must be economized. Dissemination planners should—

- Identify and select both routine and time-sensitive modes.

● Determine and prioritize both dissemination point-to-point and broadcast modes for the widest possible range of tactical situations, to include standard and alarm situations and also criteria.
● Maintain awareness of the status of all MAGTF and key external CIS plans and operations.

Allocate Resources

The commander and intelligence officer exercising centralized control of intelligence dissemination must allocate resources to ensure that the needs of subordinate commanders are properly addressed and supported. Detachments from one or more intelligence/reconnaissance/CI unit may be placed in direct support (DS) or attached to subordinate units. They may also be used to create intelligence nodes to support a subordinate unit or center (for example, the rear area operations center; civil-military operations center). This must be done in coordination with the G-3/S-3 (for unit concept of operations and tactical task organization); the G-6/S-6 (for CIS resources); the G-1/S-1 (for personnel augmentation and courier support); the G-4/S-4 (for unique intelligence element's combat service support); and within the G-2/S-2 section for effective management of dissemination personnel and assets.

Disseminate

Intelligence products must be disseminated as quickly as possible to all relevant users. Dissemination planners should anticipate overloaded or disabled communication links by planning alternate distribution means. Redundancy must be planned for and used as needed.

Good reporting and dissemination flow diagrams and matrices assist in dissemination development, planning, and execution. They also provide combat operations center (COC), P&A cell, and SARC watch personnel with references to guide them in dissemination decisions.

Considerations During Dissemination

Current Tactical Situation

The dissemination plan will provide guidance for when, to whom, and how to disseminate the various types of intelligence and products.

Disseminators must always evaluate the IR against the current tactical situation; in addition to planned recipients ask who has a need for the intelligence; and initiate necessary action.

Status of Current Communications and Information Systems Readiness

Dissemination managers must continuously monitor the status of all CIS resources and pathways, primary and alternate. Continuous coordination with the G-2/S-2 COC watch officer and the G-6/S-6's systems control (SYSCON) and technical control (TECHCON) centers is mandatory to rapidly assess problems and determine availability of alternate communication means.

Quality Control of Dissemination

Dissemination planning is generally centrally managed. Dissemination execution is decentralized and conducted by a wide variety of individuals—P&A cell, SARC, and COC intelligence personnel; intelligence, CI, and reconnaissance collectors; and even operations, fires, and other nonintelligence personnel. New CIS technologies allow greater intelligence access to and dissemination from commands and organizations external to the MAGTF as well as command echelons within the MAGTF. Additionally, the ability of users to pull information from nonmilitary or intelligence sources (for example, news media, academia, nongovernmental organizations [NGOs]) and use it as intelligence presents a quality control challenge. Data may be incorrect, misleading, dated or incomplete, excessive or wrongly perceived as conclusive. Users may use this data without understanding the basis. Detailed, well-designed standing operating procedures (SOPs) and continuous coordination are critical to successfully dealing with these challenges.

Evaluate Effectiveness

After disseminating an intelligence product, disseminators must ensure that it was received and understood by all intended recipients. Intelligence products are occasionally misrouted or not transmitted completely. Verification of receipt can be accomplished through a telephone call or email confirmation from select addressees. Follow-on contact should be made to determine if intelligence needs were met or if the provided intelligence led to any new IRs.

Train Personnel

Regular and realistic training of all intelligence personnel and users is needed to improve their understanding of dissemination operational capabilities and limitations, their tactical abilities and judgments, and their technical skills and expertise.

Intelligence dissemination capabilities must be exercised under a variety of realistic tactical scenarios and operating conditions. Training must emphasizes unit SOPs, as well as other Service, joint, and intelligence agency procedures. Training must develop the following procedures:

- Ensure that dissemination problems experienced anywhere within the MAGTF are immediately brought to the attention of the appropriate personnel for corrective action.
- Maintain awareness of the current operational status of key intelligence-related and CIS resources.
- Confirm the receipt of disseminated intelligence.
- Quickly verify that CCIRS, PIRs, and IRs have been fully satisfied, and whether they generate or affect any new IRs.
- Enable commanders, planners, and other nonintelligence personnel to pull intelligence from databases, Web sites, publications, and other intelligence resources.
- Rehearse time-sensitive dissemination procedures, to include using alternate communication means.
- Disseminate intelligence to other Services, joint, multinational forces, and NGOs.
- Integrate intelligence and reconnaissance units' intelligence, C2, and CIS operations in HQs of all subordinate organizations down to the battalion, squadron, and combat service support detachment level.
- Execute specialized and unique intelligence dissemination CIS capabilities (for example, SCI sanitization and reporting of DOD clandestine collection activities).

CHAPTER 4
INTELLIGENCE DISSEMINATION PLANNING

The MAGTF intelligence section develops and implements intelligence dissemination plans. While written from the MEF intelligence section perspective, the guidelines addressed in this chapter may be tailored to any echelon. Appendix A provides a sample intelligence dissemination plan format. Appendix B provides a sample intelligence CIS plan format. Appendix C provides an IDR planning matrix format.

Planning Factors

Intelligence dissemination plans and procedures must incorporate the following:

- IDR priorities, to include integrated linkage with ICRs and IPRs.
- Grouping IRs by type of intelligence and echelon of intended recipient.
- Anticipated IDRs.
- Preferred intelligence product.
- Primary and alternate communication means with all supported units.
- Routine and time-sensitive dissemination means and responsibilities.
- Communications security (COMSEC) considerations.
- Procedures to verify that the intelligence has been received by the intended recipients.

MAGTF Dissemination Standing Operating Procedures, Plans, and Orders

The assistant chief of staff (AC/S) G-2 has overall responsibility for MAGTF intelligence dissemination SOPs, plans, and orders. The ISC is responsible for the preparation of the intelligence dissemination plan and the intelligence CIS plan. The CM/DO is responsible for execution.

The principal intelligence CIS planning guide/tool for a MAGTF operation is tab D, Intelligence CIS Plan, to Appendix 16 (Intelligence Operations Plan) of Annex B of the OPLAN/OPORD. Other portions of Annex B, however, also include key intelligence CIS information. For example, tabs A, B, and C to Appendix 16 (respectively, the collections, production and dissemination plans); tab E (Intelligence Reports) to Appendix 16; and paragraph 5 (Intelligence C2) to Annex B of the basic plan.

In addition to Annex B, portions of Annex K (CIS) influence intelligence CIS architecture planning. The following are included:

- Appendix 14, Communications Restoration.
- Appendix 23, Task Organization/Communications Guard Shifts.
- Appendix 26, Radio Battalion/special security officer (SSO) Communications.
- Appendix 31, Communications Support for Intelligence.
- Appendix 34, Internet Protocol Assignments.
- Appendix 35, CIS Support for Information Management.

Dissemination Planning Process

Intelligence dissemination should be—

- Preplanned.
- Tailored for specific recipients based on unit mission.
- Automated to the greatest degree possible.
- Included with back-up plans and manual means of dissemination.

Identify Dissemination Requirements

Validated and prioritized CCIRs, PIRs, and IRs drive IDR planning. When identifying requirements, the four W's—who, where, what, and when—provide a usable, four-step process for identifying dissemination needs.

Who

Identify and group who may need dissemination support, not only those specifically involved with an IR. These units may include higher HQ (for example, joint task force (JTF); external intelligence units (for example, JIC, joint interrogation and debriefing center or joint document exploitation center); adjacent units (for example, United States Army units); and internal elements of the MAGTF (current operations center, force fires coordination center, rear area operations center or civil-military operations center).

Where

Where intelligence is disseminated will likely correspond to the location of the intended recipient; however, command relationships, operational phase, task-organization or other factors may determine other locations for dissemination requirements. Intelligence dissemination planners must pay particular attention to special dissemination requirements during any of the following situations:

- Intelligence support provided via reach back or involving split-base operations.
- Location of unit C2 facilities during tactical displacements.
- When the unit can utilize communications provided by a collocated unit.
- Operations afloat and ship-shore movement phases.
- Heliborne or air movement operations.
- Terrain, weather or atmospheric conditions that may affect dissemination.

What

The next step is to determine what type intelligence support (for example, finished deliberate intelligence, time-sensitive intelligence products or particular formats) each recipient requires. The who and what are cross-referenced with the following:

- Finished intelligence products (intelligence studies, estimates or reports).
- Addressee indicator groups, Defense Special Security Communications System address groups, collective address designators, and MAGTF units.
- Alarm intelligence support (for example, I&W report or time-sensitive target of opportunity reporting).
- Imagery IRs.
- Signals intelligence (SIGINT) (for example, requirement for time-sensitive/non-codeword reporting; sanitized version SCI products).
- Human intelligence (HUMINT) (for example, CI time-sensitive reports, tactical interrogation reports, special CI reporting).
- Geographic intelligence (for example, planning and operational map allowance requirements, terrain models and analyses, geospatial information needed for automated systems).
- Reconnaissance and surveillance requirements.
- Level(s) of classified information that the user requires.
- Releasability and formats for sharing intelligence with multinational units.

When

The final basic dissemination planning step is to identify timeliness requirements. In general, intelligence should be disseminated as soon as possible. Planning considerations include the following:

- Rapidly assessing the feasibility of satisfying the commander's stated LTIOV requirement.
- Nature of the IR (for example, routine, time sensitive, CCIR).

- Communication transmission means desired by the user (for example, voice, text, electronic).
- Capabilities and current status of the MAGTF CIS system.

Develop the Intelligence and Information Flow

Intelligence Flow

Dissemination planning must begin with an analysis of intelligence and information processes. Visualization of the flow of intelligence flow can contribute to detailed planning. The use of various types of flow diagrams and dissemination planning matrices can assist in the process. When building a MAGTF dissemination matrix, key dissemination recipients, such as the MSCs, must always be depicted. No standard dissemination matrix has been developed for all dissemination planning functions; however, some examples are provided in Appendix C (Intelligence Dissemination Requirements Planning Matrix) and Appendix D (Intelligence Reports Dissemination Matrix Format).

Intelligence Reporting

An intelligence report matrix depicting standard and time-sensitive reporting guidance should be prepared for every operation. The particular format will be tailored to meet unit needs. The matrix should detail the flow of intelligence reports to be prepared or handled by the intelligence section and the IOC. For MAGTF elements, this should show the flow from the original reporter (collector, SARC or P&A cell) to recipients for each type intelligence report. Appendix D shows an example of an intelligence report matrix.

IDR Planning Matrix

The IDR planning matrix is a tool that assists the CM/DO in managing the MAGTF intelligence dissemination effort. Using an IDR planning matrix helps keep the focus on the commander's decision points, PIRs, and other key IRs. This format may be tailored as needed per unit SOP. See appendix C.

Develop the Dissemination Plan

The intelligence dissemination plan must be fully integrated with MEF collections and production operations; clearly state how the intelligence will

---

EXAMPLE

Notional MEF Intelligence Support to Targeting Flow

Targeting Related IR Management. Targeting-related IRs will be submitted by higher, adjacent, and subordinate elements. These will be submitted to the CM/DO in the intelligence operations center (IOC). The CM/DO will consult with the P&A cell and other producers to determine if they can answer the request. If yes, they will do so per either the production or dissemination plan, disseminate products as appropriate, and also post the answer or the product on the intelligence homepage. If the analysts cannot answer the request, they will so notify the CM/DO who will then prioritize and request collection.

Support to Time-Sensitive Targeting. Each potential source of time-sensitive targeting intelligence must make decisions on whether the combat information received constitutes high-payoff target reporting (HPTR), and if it is targetable. Daily guidance reflecting changes to the commander's intent, G-3 force fires targeting priorities, the daily targeting board, and the G-2/IOC's PIRs, and intelligence reporting criteria provides this. A tracking and identification code/system should be established for these reports. Reactive targeting occurs when high-payoff targets (HPTs) are located. This time-sensitive intelligence is collected and disseminated through the organization responsible for reporting from the sensor concerned. Generally, information will come to the MEF G-2 and its IOC through the SARC or the COC intelligence watch (point of contact for friendly unit intelligence and combat information reporting). In special cases and when authorized, this flow may be direct from a specialized intelligence unit to designated recipients (for example, from the radio battalion's operational control and analysis center to the COC).

Immediate Dissemination of High-Value Target Reporting. If the information is not an HPT or battle damage assessment (BDA) report, it is moved to the P&A cell for analysis. The P&A cell will review all reports to determine if they are high-value, time-sensitive intelligence. If yes, it will note who needs to see it and immediately disseminate it per the dissemination plan and intelligence reporting criteria. If no, it will determine who needs to see it, internal to the G-2, for use in subsequent intelligence P&AO.

Analysis and Dissemination of Intelligence Products. P&A cell analysts will process the information against the current and estimated future enemy situation using other relevant intelligence and databases as appropriate. Time-sensitive intelligence will rapidly be incorporated by the analyst into an intelligence report that is disseminated immediately per the dissemination plan and current reporting criteria. Where immediate dissemination is not required, the analyst will likely forward the intelligence for possible inclusion in the intelligence summary or other intelligence products. Where targets are developed through the analytical process, the analysts will forward all targets to P&A cell's target analysis/BDA team for follow-on support to the targeting process.

be delivered to the requestor; and be flexible enough to adapt to ongoing tactical developments. The dissemination plan must determine both the physical means of dissemination and procedures to be followed in transmission.

Design and Coordinate the Dissemination Architecture

An intelligence dissemination architecture should be designed schematically so that it depicts links from the source to the recipient. It should depict organizations, intelligence systems, and CIS connectivity among the forces' intelligence collectors/producers and the supported decision makers/planners and C2 nodes. It must encompass the different types of intelligence support, from higher HQ produced all-source intelligence through time-sensitive tactical intelligence information. To account for different types of data and intelligence, several linkages may need to be constructed. It must also depict both primary and alternate channels for standard and broadcast dissemination. The following must be incorporated:

- Detail the various means for dissemination: digital networks, radio, wire, and courier communications channels, to include MAGTF common as well as dedicated intelligence systems and architectures.
- Provide primary and alternate plans for standard, alarm, supply-push, and demand-pull capabilities.
- Account for different types of data forms and intelligence, to include that requiring special or unique security controls (for example, SCI).

The ISC has principal staff responsibility for the dissemination architecture. IDR architecture needs should be stated within the broader intelligence C2 and CIS requirements, approved by the G-2 and the commander, and then provided in a prioritized list to appropriate G-3/S-3, G-5/S-5, and G-6/S-6 planners. Tailored copies may also be provided to higher and subordinate intelligence officers to support collaborative detailed planning.

Establish Dissemination Procedures

Dissemination procedures should be established for the delivery of intelligence from producers. The precedence of transmission (for example, routine and flash) should be agreed upon by all involved parties in advance. Audiences should be predetermined by defining broadcast parameters. Reporting thresholds and filters should be identified early.

Plan and Manage the Common Tactical Picture, Common Operational Picture

The dissemination of common tactical picture (CTP) track data, its subsequent processing, and further dissemination must be planned for, monitored, and managed. Track management procedures must be established to achieve a useful CTP within the higher level common operational picture (COP) environment. Each echelon of command, beginning at the tactical maneuver battalion/aviation squadron level, reports and manages the track database for its own units and those attached or in DS. Track data should be auto-forwarded via broadcast up to the next higher echelon until it reaches the MAGTF CE. Once correlated, track data is rebroadcast back down to each subsequent echelon as the MAGTF CTP. As track data is updated it automatically updates each echelon database and CTP. This dissemination process must be carefully managed.

Communications Security

The effective dissemination of intelligence requires secure communication means. COMSEC planning considerations include the following:

- Coordinate with the appointed SSOs in all units authorized to receive and use SCI.
- Adhere to SCI security handling, processing, and storage requirements.

- Obtain authority and establish procedures for the sanitization of SCI products, reports, and other information.
- Determine and coordinate SCI and GENSER LANs and WANs.
- Determine and coordinate both SCI and GENSER courier requirements and operations.
- Determine COMSEC materiel system requirements for intelligence and SCI communications.
- Determine communication requirements between sensitive compartmented information facilities (SCIFs), tactical sensitive compartmented information facilities (TSCIFs), supporting security forces, and supported units.

Allocate Resources

The intelligence officer, in coordination with the unit's communications officer, should allocate available personnel and equipment resources to support the dissemination requested. Requirements must be estimated and resources allocated for routine and time-sensitive operations, with sufficient redundant capabilities for each.

Monitor Execution

A wide range of intelligence dissemination will be occurring simultaneously. It is critical to constantly evaluate its effectiveness, the quality of support provided to commanders, and rapidly identify and resolve problems as follows:

- Develop a dissemination tracking matrix to record receipt of major and/or critical intelligence and products by intended recipients. (See fig. 4-1)
- Determine if the user is satisfied with the quality and quantity of intelligence.
- Supervise adherence to specified dissemination priorities and reporting criteria.
- Ensure that no precedence abuse exists or information overload occurs to degrade or overload communication channels.

Maintain awareness of the operational status of all supporting CIS, as well as the status of PIRs, IRs, and IDRs, to rapidly make necessary changes consistent with ongoing operations.

Unit	Watch Officer		HQ BN		G-1		TAC UNIT		MOBILE		G-3		G-4		G-6		2d Mar		6th Mar
PRODUCT	sent	rec	sent	rec	sent	rec	sent	rec	sent	rec	sent	rec	sent	rec	sent	rec	sent	rec	sent

Figure 4-1. Sample Dissemination Tracking Matrix.

CHAPTER 5
INTELLIGENCE ESTIMATES AND STUDIES

Intelligence estimates, studies, reports, and briefings are the principal intelligence products disseminated during MAGTF operations. Detailed information on preparing each is contained in MCWP 2-12, *MAGTF Intelligence Production and Analysis*.

Dissemination

Disseminating intelligence estimates and studies provides large amounts of detailed data in support of general operational planning. Many estimates and studies are scheduled production documents; however, estimates and studies may be produced and distributed quickly during a rapidly developing crisis. Intelligence estimates and studies may be disseminated via paper copy or a computer diskette mailed to a predetermined distribution list or electronically via a secure datalink. In most cases, broader dissemination will be possible by posting these products on Web pages accessible by the intended recipient.

Advantages versus Disadvantages

Intelligence estimates and studies are often accompanied by overlays, color graphics, and other aids in a standardized format. Once disseminated, these documents are available for continuous reference. But while intelligence estimates and studies can serve as invaluable background references, they require significant time and resources to produce. These products are prepared with a specific information cut-off time and may be difficult to update quickly. In a crisis, intelligence estimates and studies may be difficult to reproduce mechanically for rapid dissemination to all necessary subordinate units.

Reproduction or reformatting of imagery and geospatial information materials can be particularly difficult.

Intelligence Estimate

The intelligence estimate is the primary means for providing basic and current intelligence and results of the intelligence preparation of the battlespace (IPB) effort focused on a specific mission. It is usually the first significant intelligence product developed to support initial orientation, immediate mission analysis, and other planning needs. The scope and detail of the estimate will be determined by the following:

- Resources of the command preparing it.
- Nature of the operation.
- Available intelligence.
- Identified IRs.
- Prior contingency planning.
- Time and resources available.

The intelligence estimate should be succinct, yet provide commanders and staffs the necessary intelligence for planning and early decisionmaking. A summary of basic intelligence, the estimate normally uses supporting studies for in-depth treatment of specific aspects of the enemy situation or the area of operations (AO). Whenever possible, the intelligence estimate should clearly present the analysis and conclusions developed during IPB. When contained in an OPLAN or OPORD, the intelligence estimate is typically found in Appendix 11 to Annex B. The finished estimate may be written, graphic or verbal in form. Subparagraphs and tabs may be added and omitted, based on their relevance to the stated mission. For topics that require a large amount of data, information and intelligence (for example, beaches, weapons capabilities, and technical characteristics), the salient facts, and conclusions should be summarized in the body of the estimate with details included as a tab(s).

MAGTF Contingency Intelligence Study

This is a baseline intelligence study prepared in advance for standing OPLANs and likely contingencies. It is based on the intelligence estimate format and can be updated relatively quickly and converted into an intelligence estimate when an alert or warning order is received.

Intelligence Studies

Intelligence studies deliver detailed intelligence on specific aspects of the AO or threat (for example, beaches, minefields, helicopter landing zones (HLZ)s, hydrography or airfields). Studies directly support intelligence estimates. Wherever possible, standardized formats should be used and essential intelligence should be transformed into graphics. Unit intelligence studies should be disseminated at least two echelons upward and downward, especially if the intelligence contained in the study is derived from organic collection assets.

Target/Objective Studies

Target/objective studies are focused, detailed intelligence products that aid in the application of fires or the maneuver of forces against a specific target set or area. These studies can also be used by small units for mission preparation and execution. Target/objective studies are graphically oriented and may use many of the graphics derived during the IPB process. This intelligence product provides tailored, detailed, mission-specific intelligence in support of small unit execution. It usually consists of text descriptions that are supported by graphics. Graphics may include annotated imagery, map enhancements, terrain models, blueprints, diagrams, and schematics. Target folders contain textual descriptions and graphics, but annotated imagery, map enhancements, diagrams, schematics, and mapping products are key elements. In a tactical situation, target intelligence becomes highly perishable and must be disseminated as quickly as possible to controlling, coordinating, and delivering units.

Intelligence Preparation of the Battlespace Products

IPB is a continuous, systemic process of analyzing the threat and environment presented in the intelligence estimate. IPB products provide supported commanders and planners with a graphic portrayal of the battlespace. By integrating, analyzing, evaluating, interpreting, and fusing vast amounts of textual information into symbols, IPB products convey easily understood overlays to operators and planners with detailed intelligence available in supporting text products or intelligence databases. Overlays, such as the modified combined obstacle and fields of fire overlays, quickly and effectively depict such key terrain and enemy characteristics as mobility corridors, obstacles, terrain trafficability, and threat COAs. IPB overlay updates should always be disseminated as rapidly as possible to other staff sections and subordinate units.

Standardized formats for IPB products should be used to the maximum extent possible and tailored according to the situation or a user's unique needs.

CHAPTER 6
INTELLIGENCE BRIEFINGS

The ability to prepare and convey intelligence in a clear, concise manner is an essential skill for intelligence personnel. For the operational intelligence officer, the briefings will be the most common way to disseminate intelligence to the command. However, intelligence personnel at all command levels frequently use intelligence briefings, formal and informal, to disseminate intelligence to commanders, staffs, and others.

Intelligence briefings are used to convey information in a concise, mission-oriented format. Depending on available preparation time, briefing styles can range from formal presentations with detailed hand-outs and graphics to concise verbal updates.

Dissemination

In nontactical situations, given sufficient lead-time, formal briefings can be supplemented with multimedia products. During operations, intelligence can be relayed rapidly through short verbal updates. To convey a large amount of intelligence, paper hand-outs, electronic presentations, graphics or other supplemental material covering key briefing points may accompany the verbal presentation.

The intelligence brief should focus on the intelligence and events that correspond to the CCIRs and other PIRs. Doing so ensures that the commander is given the most essential information in the shortest amount of time. This does not preclude additional information being presented. If something of significance occurs that affects the current or future plans, the commander must be informed. Good judgment must prevail.

Advantages versus Disadvantages

Briefings are an effective way to disseminate intelligence quickly. They permit interaction with the user and allow the user to provide instant feedback to the briefer on content and conclusions or to ask questions. Preparation for briefings can be time-consuming, however; and briefings usually reach only a selected audience, such as the commander's staff.

Information Brief

The most common form of briefing is the information brief. Its primary purposes are initial situation orientation for planning and enhancing situational awareness and understanding. Common examples are the initial staff orientation brief, the commander's daily update, intelligence update, intelligence estimate of supportability, mission/target intelligence brief, and the technical intelligence brief.

Initial Staff Orientation Brief

The initial staff intelligence orientation brief disseminates important characteristics of the AO and the threat. Its goal is to indoctrinate key personnel to the overall intelligence perspective concerning an impending operation and to rapidly focus commanders and key planners on mission critical factors. The initial intelligence orientation brief should generally follow the intelligence estimate format, supplying all relevant intelligence on the AO and the enemy. Much of the content of this type briefing is derived from higher-echelon studies and estimates and is presented as basic background intelligence. Because this type briefing can easily become too long or too detailed for timely dissemination, graphics should be used wherever possible.

Commander's Daily Update Brief

Morning or evening update briefs may be formal and detailed. They are scheduled for set times once or twice per day. Intelligence may be only part of the overall briefing. The intelligence topics include the following:

- The current situation and significant events.
- CCIRs, PIRs, and IRs.
- Collection, production, and dissemination plans and their status.
- Weather.
- Estimates of future threat actions.
- At a minimum, most likely and most dangerous enemy COAs.

Intelligence Update Brief

The intelligence update brief reviews intelligence activity since the last briefing, presents the current intelligence situation, and estimates anticipated enemy activities that may affect friendly COAs. Intelligence updates are usually scheduled briefings and are designed to address predetermined periods of time such as every 12 or 24 hours. Examples include watch turnover briefs in the unit COC, IOC or SARC. The intelligence update brief follows a temporal outline, commencing with the reporting of any significant enemy activity, including any enemy losses since the last update. It presents the current enemy situation, followed by weather forecasts, as well as intelligence estimates of enemy COAs and activity during the next reporting period. The update should also address friendly intelligence collection, production, and dissemination operations.

Intelligence Estimate of Supportability

An intelligence estimate of supportability briefing evaluates friendly COAs based on the capabilities and limitations of organic and supporting intelligence, counterintelligence, and reconnaissance forces. Its goal is to assist the commander in understanding intelligence operations capabilities, with all other friendly functional capabilities, to decide the most promising friendly COA and to identify IRs. The intelligence estimate of supportability brief addresses key factors identified by intelligence personnel that may influence friendly intelligence operations that include the following:

- Terrain.
- Weather.
- Current political situation.
- Possible reactions from the civilian populace.
- Enemy's relative strengths and weaknesses.
- Susceptibility to friendly deception or psychological operations.

The briefing addresses enemy COAs, analyzes enemy COAs versus friendly COAs based on the key factors, identifies the preferred friendly COA, and offers any other recommendations to the commander.

Mission/Target Intelligence Brief

The mission/target intelligence brief provides detailed and tailored intelligence to support execution of a specific mission. The mission/target intelligence brief has no prescribed format but should contain all pertinent intelligence impacting on a specific mission or target. Normally, this type briefing provides any intelligence and other information on activity occurring or expected to occur within a predetermined radius from a target or mission area and within a predetermined amount of time from mission execution. At a minimum, it should include an area orientation and detailed descriptions of entry points, the objective area, and the expected threat, including enemy locations, dispositions, capabilities, and vulnerabilities. Graphics should be employed extensively to portray potential enemy strengths, vulnerabilities, and potential COAs.

Technical Intelligence Brief

The technical intelligence brief provides detailed intelligence on a specific enemy weapon system, piece of equipment or functional capability and limitations. This type of briefing disseminates a substantial amount of technical and scientific intelligence in a condensed format. The technical intelligence brief has no prescribed form but should, at a minimum, provide a detailed description of the threat or weapon system and its attendant characteristics, capabilities, and vulnerabilities. If the system has associated unique visual or electronic signatures, ensure all known operating parameters are disseminated to intelligence, targeting, and key maneuver personnel. The briefing should also describe how the enemy employs the system (for example, tactics, processes, and procedures) and where it is currently deployed (for example, order of battle). Graphics should be used wherever possible to quickly convey this type of complex information.

CHAPTER 7
INTELLIGENCE REPORTS

Intelligence reports disseminate intelligence quickly to a wide audience for immediate use. Because reports contain sensitive information, they are usually transmitted by a secure communication means. Intelligence reports should be disseminated in accordance with either collection or reporting criteria or the dissemination plan. MCWP 2-12 and other MCWP and MCRP intelligence series publications provide the basic formats for these reports.

Summary Intelligence Reports

Summary intelligence reports provide the commander with an overview of significant enemy activity within a specified period of time and project anticipated enemy actions during the next reporting period. Summary reports are usually scheduled products disseminated at specific times as dictated by unit SOPs or OPLANS/OPORDs. Standard summary reports, disseminated at scheduled times, are well-suited for demand-pull dissemination, such as being posted on the MAGTF secure TDN.

Intelligence Summary

The intelligence summary (INTSUM) is a text-based or text and graphic intelligence report that provides a summary of the intelligence situation covering a specific period, normally prescribed by the unit SOP for intelligence or the intelligence annex to the OPORD (for a MEF-level operation, typically every 12 or 24 hours). It is used to report threat activities, changes to threat capabilities, and the results of further P&A. It is designed to update the original and subsequent intelligence estimates. INTSUM distribution will be in accordance with the dissemination

plan, but generally will be disseminated at least to immediate higher and subordinate commands. Using the basic format, units can tailor the INTSUM to fit the situation. With new automated information systems, INTSUMs are increasingly produced in graphic form and posted on networks for wide dissemination, with links to detailed supporting intelligence products, reports, and databases. The graphic INTSUM is maintained on computer screens linked to intelligence databases or on conventional maps with displayed/accessible supporting information.

Daily Intelligence Summary

A daily intelligence summary (DISUM) is a report prepared in message form at the JTF HQ that provides higher, lateral, and subordinate headquarters with a summary of all significant intelligence produced during the previous 24-hour period. The "as of" time for the information, content, and submission time for the report will be as specified by the joint force commander. (JP 1-02)

At higher command levels, particularly JTFs and unified commands, a DISUM will usually be published every 24 hours. While INTSUMs, particularly at lower tactical echelons, provide a tactical perspective, the DISUM is broader in scope, potentially encompasses more aspects of the threat country's elements of national power, and focuses on operational-level intelligence analysis and estimates. MAGTF command elements tasked as JTF HQ will generally be required to submit DISUMs to the combatant command HQ. See the combatant command's tactics, techniques, and procedures for the DISUM format. Although generally the same, formats may vary from theater to theater.

Periodic Intelligence Summary

The periodic intelligence summary (PERINTSUM) is a report of the intelligence situation in a tactical operation (normally produced at corps level or its equivalent and higher) usually at intervals of 24 hours or as directed by the commander. (JP 1-02)

The PERINTSUM is an expanded INTSUM covering a greater period of time as dictated by the commander. It is a means for disseminating more detailed intelligence than that provided in INTSUMs or DISUMs. PERINTSUMs are normally issued by the MAGTF CE for dissemination to higher, lower, and adjacent commands. Subordinate units may also be tasked to prepare them if directed by the commander. The format for PERINTSUMs generally is the same as used for DISUMs.

Specialized Intelligence Reports

Specialized reports include event-driven intelligence reports, such as size, activity, location, unit, time, and equipment (SALUTE) reports, and various intelligence discipline-unique intelligence reports, such as tactical electronic intelligence reports, initial photographic intelligence reports, CI spot reports, surf observation reports, and bridge reports. The purpose of generating event-driven intelligence reports is to disseminate significant intelligence to the commander or to intelligence operations personnel that could immediately alter the tactical situation or to support situation development. Event-driven and other specialized intelligence reports are disseminated as required.

Intelligence Report

The intelligence report is a standardized report that is prepared and disseminated based on its importance to the current situation rather than on a specific time schedule. It is the primary means for transmitting new and significant intelligence when facts influencing threat capabilities have been observed or when a change in threat capabilities has taken place. It is prepared at all echelons by the first intelligence element acquiring the information and forming the intelligence estimate, and is disseminated as rapidly as possible to all units that need the reported information. It may be prepared on any item of intelligence, regardless of source. Each report will concern only a single item of interest.

Battle Damage Assessment Reporting

The intelligence officer (at the MEF CE level, the ISC) ensures BDA reports conform to the OPLAN, report the nature of damage inflicted or unit/systems destroyed, and assess the degree of mission success as it relates to the initial objective. When possible, BDA reporting includes the physical damage assessment (PDA) and an analysis of the consequence of the damage on the threat unit.

At each echelon, the intelligence officer compiles, refines, and validates the various sources of BDA and develops consolidated PDAs and/or combat strength assessments. Commands will forward consolidated BDA reporting of their subordinates. MSCs will typically forward a summary BDA report to the MEF, usually covering set time periods.

At the MEF level, the P&A company, intelligence battalion, is responsible for adjusting the master order of battle databases to reflect threat combat losses. The BDA cell will prepare and disseminate formal Phase I BDA reports in accordance with theater and national policies and procedures. See MCWP 2-12 for information on BDA analysis and reporting.

Mission Report

Mission reports (MISREPs) are used by aviation units to report significant results of aircraft missions and nonimagery sightings along flight routes. They employ a standardized format that includes air task/mission number or nickname, location identifiers, time on target/time of sighting, results/sighting information, and remarks. Upon completion of post-flight debriefing, squadron S-2s should disseminate MISREPs to the MAGTF G-2/S-2 by the most expeditious means possible.

Response to a Request for Intelligence

Responses to a request for intelligence (RRFIs) are nonscheduled products designed to fill gaps in knowledge identified by subordinate tactical units. RRFIs should be answered and disseminated as quickly as possible.

Intelligence Reports Plan and Matrix

Detailed guidance and instructions for dissemination of intelligence reports must be established to ensure effective, efficient, and accurate intelligence dissemination. This may be accomplished through the use of an intelligence report matrix. The CM/DO develops and updates dissemination procedures, architectures, and reporting matrixes. The intelligence report matrix is an exhibit to the intelligence reports tab to Annex B of intelligence OPLAN/OPORD. Report matrixes may be adjusted by unit SOP. See appendix D for a sample format.

APPENDIX A
MAGTF INTELLIGENCE DISSEMINATION PLAN
APPENDIX FORMAT

Tab C (Intelligence Dissemination Plan) to Appendix 16 (Intelligence Operations Plan) to Annex B (Intelligence) explains how intelligence dissemination elements supporting the MAGTF will be used to support the operation.

CLASSIFICATION

Copy no. ___ of ___ copies
ISSUING HEADQUARTERS
PLACE OF ISSUE
Date/time group
Message reference number

TAB C TO APPENDIX 16 (INTELLIGENCE OPERATIONS PLAN) TO
ANNEX B (INTELLIGENCE) TO MAGTF OPORD X (U)
INTELLIGENCE DISSEMINATION PLAN (U)

(U) REFERENCES: Identify organic DOD; Director, National Security Agency; National Imagery and Mapping Agency, and other directives; combatant commander, JTF, joint force maritime component commander/joint force land component commander/joint force air component commander or other higher authorities' OPORDs, tactics, techniques, and procedures), and SOPs for intelligence dissemination operations; intelligence reporting formats or any other relevant documents that pertain to anticipated intelligence dissemination operations.

1. (U) Situation

   a. (U) Define the AO and Area of Interest. Describe the limits of the AO and area of interest. Summarize pertinent weather, terrain, and other AO characteristics and conditions as they may influence the conduct of intelligence dissemination operations.

   b. (U) Enemy. Refer to Annex B (Intelligence) and current intelligence estimates for threat capabilities, limitations, vulnerabilities, and order of battle pertinent to intelligence dissemination operations.

Page number

CLASSIFICATION

CLASSIFICATION

c. (U) <u>Assigned MAGTF Organic and Supporting Intelligence Dissemination Assets</u>. Identify organic and supporting forces available to perform intelligence dissemination functions.

d. (U) <u>Assumptions</u>. (Derived during the mission analysis step of the Marine Corps Planning Process.)

e. (U) <u>Intelligence Dissemination Considerations</u>. List key intelligence dissemination, CIS and interoperability considerations that impact this OPLAN/OPORD.

(1) (U) Availability of national and commercial intelligence and multipurpose CIS resources.

(2) (U) Intelligence C2 and dissemination support to and from JTF or component HQ and other external commands and/or intelligence organizations.

(3) (U) Creation and manning of forward intelligence C2 and operations elements.

2. (U) <u>Mission</u>. State concisely the intelligence dissemination mission as it relates to the command's planned operations.

3. (U) <u>Execution</u>

a. (U) <u>Concept of Operations</u>. Summarize command relationships, task-organization, main and supporting efforts, and the scope of MAGTF and supporting intelligence dissemination operations. Reference the unit's intelligence SOP and Appendix 16 (Intelligence Operations Plan) to Annex B. Restate as appropriate the commander's intent and pertinent aspects of the unit's overall concept of operations as they relate to intelligence operations. Outline the purpose and concept of intelligence dissemination operations, specified priorities, and summarize the means and agencies to be employed to support the operations and intelligence concepts of operations. Address the integration of JTF, other components, theater, national, and allied intelligence operations, dissemination, and CIS support.

b. (U) <u>Dissemination Tasks for Intelligence Units and Organizations, Subordinate Units, and Detachment Commanders/Officers in Charge</u>.

(1) (U) <u>Orders to Subordinate, Attached, and Supporting Units</u>. Use separate subparagraphs to list detailed instructions for each unit conducting intelligence-related dissemination operations, including the originating HQ, subordinate commands, and separate intelligence support units.

CLASSIFICATION

CLASSIFICATION

(a) (U) Marine division(s).

(b) (U) Marine aircraft wing(s).

(c) (U) Force service support group(s).

(d) (U) Commanding officer, intelligence battalion/intelligence support coordinator.

    <u>1</u> (U) Officer in charge (OIC), support cell.

    <u>2</u> (U) OIC, P&A cell.

    <u>3</u> (U) OIC, surveillance and reconnaissance cell.

    <u>4</u> (U) Intelligence systems officer.

    <u>5</u> (U) Commanding officer, CI/HUMINT company.

    <u>6</u> (U) Platoon commander, imagery intelligence platoon.

    <u>7</u> (U) Platoon commander, topographic platoon.

    <u>8</u> (U) OIC, joint surveillance target attack radar system common ground station.

(e) (U) Commanding officer, Marine unmanned aerial vehicle squadron.

(f) (U) Commanding officer, Marine tactical electronic warfare squadron.

(g) (U) Commanding officer, radio battalion.

(h) (U) Commanding officer, force reconnaissance company.

(i) (U) OIC, national intelligence support team (if attached).

(2) (U) <u>Requests to Higher, Adjacent, and Cooperating Units</u>. Provide separate numbered subparagraphs pertaining to each unit not organic, attached or supporting and from which intelligence dissemination support is requested, including other components, JTF HQ, allied or coalition forces, theater, and national operational and intelligence elements.

Page number

CLASSIFICATION

CLASSIFICATION

c. (U) <u>Coordinating Instructions</u>. Reference Appendix 16 (Intelligence Operations Plan), Annex K (CIS), Annex J (C2), as well as command, other unit, intelligence and CI SOPs. Detail here or in supporting tabs key changes to unit SOPs. Additional topics to include are as follows:

- Requesting dissemination support.
- Timely reporting procedures for intelligence CIS problems.
- Coordinating switchover to backup dissemination paths.
- Intelligence operations.
- C2.
- CIS hand over between command echelons.

(1) (U) <u>General Dissemination Guidance and Procedures</u>. Use separate subparagraphs to list detailed instructions for routine and time-sensitive dissemination, precedence of transmissions, predetermined recipient lists, general and specific broadcast parameters, reporting thresholds and reporting filters.

(2) (U) <u>Intelligence Reporting Criteria</u>

(3) (U) <u>Resource Allocation</u>. Discuss dissemination resource allocation between the main and supporting efforts, and between support to current operations and support to future operations.

(4) (U) <u>Intranet Management</u>. List detailed instructions for homepage and database management, to include authorities for posting, updating, and removing information and intelligence.

(5) (U) <u>Common Operational Picture/Common Tactical Picture</u>. List detailed instructions for track data and auto-forwarding, broadcast times, and boundary/track ownership responsibilities.

(6) (U) <u>Formats and Standardization</u>. Provide formats for internal and external MAGTF intelligence dissemination and reporting, preformatted templates and/or where to find these referenced elsewhere in the OPORD. Include standards and limits on size and composition of files attached to electronic mail.

CLASSIFICATION

CLASSIFICATION

4. (U) <u>Administration and Logistics</u>

    a. (U) <u>Logistics</u>. Reference Annex D (Logistics). Identify intelligence dissemination logistics requirements and concerns, such as follows:

- Unique combat service support requirements (batteries, unique replacement parts).
- Procedures, and other guidance to support MAGTF intelligence units and operations.
- Procedures for specialized technical logistics support necessary from external organizations.
- Map distribution.
- Requirements for courier runs.

    b. (U) <u>Personnel</u>. Identify personnel requirements and concerns that affect intelligence dissemination operations and support (systems administrators or global sourcing requirements).

5. (U) <u>Command and Control</u>

    a. (U) <u>Command Relationships</u>. Reference Annex J (Command Relationships). Provide any instructions necessary regarding MAGTF command relationships that will influence intelligence operations and dissemination support.

    b. (U) <u>Information Management</u>. Reference Annex U (Information Management), Annex C (Operations) and Appendix 16 (Intelligence Operations Plan). Provide any instructions necessary regarding information management (time-sensitive and routine reporting criteria, intelligence databases, reports) that will influence MAGTF intelligence dissemination, reporting, and other operations.

    c. (U) <u>Communications and Information Systems</u>. Reference Appendix 16 (Intelligence Operations Plan) and Annex K (CIS). Provide any instructions necessary regarding CIS that will influence MAGTF intelligence dissemination operations. List intelligence dissemination priorities (by operational phase, intelligence units, operational intelligence and C2 nodes, and intelligence activities. Choose the most effective approach for the operation.

CLASSIFICATION

d. (U) <u>Intelligence C2 Nodes and Facilities</u>. Reference the unit's SOP and Appendix 16 (Intelligence Operations Plan). Provide any guidance and instructions necessary regarding establishment and operation of intelligence C2 nodes and facilities and dissemination support and priorities to these to include as follows:

- G-2/S-2 elements within future plans.
- Future operations.
- Current operations, and force fires centers.
- IOC's support cell.
- SARC and P&A cell.
- CI/HUMINT company command post.
- Reconnaissance operations center.
- Operations control and analysis center.
- Command element tactical or rear echelons.
- Intelligence liaison elements.

TABS:
A Intelligence Dissemination Flow Diagram(s)
B Intelligence Dissemination Requirements Matrix

CLASSIFICATION

APPENDIX B
INTELLIGENCE COMMUNICATIONS AND INFORMATION SYSTEMS PLAN APPENDIX FORMAT

Tab D (Intelligence CIS Plan) to Appendix 16 (Intelligence Operations Plan) to Annex B (Intelligence) explains how intelligence CIS elements supporting the MAGTF will be used to support the operation.

CLASSIFICATION

Copy no. __ of __ copies
Copy no. ___ of ___ copies
ISSUING HEADQUARTERS
PLACE OF ISSUE
Date/time group
Message reference number

Tab D TO APPENDIX 16 (INTELLIGENCE OPERATIONS PLAN) TO ANNEX B (INTELLIGENCE) TO MAGTF OPORD X (U)
INTELLIGENCE COMMUNICATIONS AND INFORMATION SYSTEMS PLAN (U)

REFERENCES: Identify organic DOD; Director, National Security Agency; National Imagery and Mapping Agency; and other directives; combatant commander, JTF, joint force maritime component commander/joint force land component commander/joint force air component commander or other higher authorities' OPORDS, TTP, and SOP for intelligence CIS operations; formats; and any other relevant documents that pertain to anticipated intelligence operations.

1. (U) Situation

   a. (U) Define the AO and Area of Interest. Describe the limits of the AO and area of interest. Summarize pertinent weather, terrain, and other AO characteristics and conditions as they may influence the conduct of intelligence CIS operations.

   b. (U) Enemy. Refer to Annex B (Intelligence) and current intelligence estimates for threat capabilities, limitations, vulnerabilities, and order of battle pertinent to intelligence CIS operations.

CLASSIFICATION

CLASSIFICATION

c. (U) <u>Assigned MAGTF Organic and Supporting Intelligence CIS Assets</u>. Identify organic and supporting forces available to perform C2 or intelligence CIS functions.

d. (U) <u>Assumptions</u>. Derived during the mission analysis step of the Marine Corps planning process.

e. (U) <u>Intelligence CIS Considerations</u>. List key intelligence CIS and interoperability considerations that impact this OPLAN/OPORD.

(1) (U) Availability of national and commercial intelligence and multipurpose CIS resources.

(2) (U) Intelligence C2 and dissemination support to and from JTF/component HQ and other external commands and intelligence organizations.

(3) (U) Creation and manning of forward intelligence C2 and operations elements.

2. (U) <u>MISSION</u>. State concisely the intelligence CIS mission as it relates to the command's planned operations.

3. (U) <u>Execution</u>

a. (U) <u>Concept of Operations</u>. Summarize command relationships, task organization, main and supporting efforts, and the scope of MAGTF and supporting intelligence CIS operations. Reference the unit's intelligence SOP and Appendix 16 (Intelligence Operations Plan) to Annex B. Restate as appropriate the commander's intent and pertinent aspects of the unit's overall concept of operations as they relate to intelligence operations. Outline the purpose and concept of intelligence CIS operations, specified priorities, and summarize the means and agencies to be employed to support the operations and intelligence concepts of operations. Address the integration of JTF, other components, theater, national, and allied intelligence operations and CIS support.

b. (U) <u>CIS Tasks for Intelligence Units and Organizations, Subordinate Units, and Detachment Commanders/Officers in Charge</u>.

(1) (U) <u>Orders to Subordinate, Attached, and Supporting Units</u>. Use separate sub-paragraphs to list detailed instructions for each unit conducting intelligence-related dissemination operations, including the originating HQ, subordinate commands, and separate intelligence support units.

Page number

CLASSIFICATION

CLASSIFICATION

(a) (U) Marine division(s).

(b) (U) Marine aircraft wing(s).

(c) (U) Force service support group(s).

(d) (U) Commanding officer, intelligence battalion/intelligence support coordinator.

    <u>1</u> (U) OIC, support cell.

    <u>2</u> (U) OIC, P&A cell.

    <u>3</u> (U) OIC, SARC.

    <u>4</u> (U) Intelligence systems officer.

    <u>5</u> (U) Commanding officer, CI/HUMINT company.

    <u>6</u> (U) Platoon commander, imagery intelligence platoon.

    <u>7</u> (U) Platoon commander, topographic platoon.

    <u>8</u> (U) OIC, joint surveillance target attack radar system common ground station.

(e) (U) Commanding officer, Marine unmanned aerial vehicle squadron.

(f) (U) Commanding officer, Marine tactical electronic warfare squadron.

(g) (U) Commanding officer, radio battalion.

(h) (U) Commanding officer, force reconnaissance company.

(i) (U) OIC, national intelligence support team (if attached).

(2) (U) <u>Requests to Higher, Adjacent, and Cooperating Units</u>. Provide separate numbered subparagraphs pertaining to each unit not organic, attached or supporting and from which intelligence CIS support is requested, including other components, JTF HQ, allied or coalition forces, theater, and national operational and intelligence elements.

CLASSIFICATION

CLASSIFICATION

c. (U) <u>Coordinating Instructions</u>. Reference Appendix 16 (Intelligence Operations Plan), Annex K (CIS), Annex J (C2), and command, other unit, intelligence and CI SOPs. Detail here or in supporting tabs key changes to unit SOPs. Additional topics to include are as follows:

- Requesting CIS support.
- Timely reporting procedures for intelligence CIS problems.
- Coordinating switchover to backup dissemination paths.
- Intelligence operations.
- C2.
- CIS hand over between command echelons.

4. (U) <u>Administration and Logistics</u>

a. (U) <u>Logistics</u>. Reference Annex D (Logistics). Identify intelligence CIS logistics requirements and concerns, such as follows:

- Unique combat service support requirements (batteries, unique replacement art).
- Procedures, and other guidance to support MAGTF intelligence units and operations.
- Procedures for specialized technical logistics support necessary from external organizations.
- Requirements for courier runs.

b. (U) <u>Personnel</u>. Identify personnel requirements and concerns that affect intelligence CIS operations and support (systems administrators, global sourcing requirements).

5. (U) <u>Command and Control</u>

a. (U) <u>Command Relationships</u>. Reference Annex J (Command Relationships). Provide any instructions necessary regarding MAGTF command relationships that will influence intelligence operations and CIS support.

b. (U) <u>Information Management</u>. Reference Annex U (Information Management), Annex C (Operations) and Appendix 16 (Intelligence Operations Plan). Provide any instructions necessary regarding information management (time-sensitive and routine reporting criteria, intelligence databases, reports) that will influence MAGTF intelligence CIS, reporting, and other operations.

Page number

CLASSIFICATION

CLASSIFICATION

c. (U) <u>Communications and Information Systems</u>. Reference Appendix 16 (Intelligence Operations Plan) and Annex K (CIS). Provide any instructions necessary regarding CIS that will influence MAGTF intelligence dissemination operations. List intelligence CIS priorities by operational phase, intelligence units, intelligence operations and C2 nodes, and intelligence activities. Use the most effective approach for the operation.

d. (U) <u>Intelligence C2 Nodes and Facilities</u>. Reference the unit's SOP and Appendix 16 (Intelligence Operations Plan). Provide any guidance and instructions necessary regarding establishment and operation of intelligence C2 nodes and facilities and CIS support and priorities to these to include as follows:

- G-2/S-2 elements within future plans.
- Future operations.
- Current operations, and force fires centers.
- IOC's support cell.
- SARC and P&A cell.
- CI/HUMINT company command post.
- Reconnaissance operations center.
- Operations control and analysis center.
- Command element tactical or rear echelons.
- Intelligence liaison elements.

TABS:

A Intelligence CIS Architecture Diagrams

- Include an diagram for the overall, overarching intelligence CIS architecture.
- Include diagrams by intelligence discipline (imagery intelligence, signals intelligence, HUMINT) if possible and useful for the operation.
- Include blueprints and CIS wire diagrams for all intelligence C2 and operations nodes and facilities, as appropriate.

B Intelligence Information Management Flow Diagram(s)

CLASSIFICATION

APPENDIX C
SAMPLE INTELLIGENCE DISSEMINATION
REQUIREMENTS PLANNING MATRIX

The sample IDR planning matrix is developed to assist in dissemination planning and includes the following information.

Requestor: identify the unit name or staff section that requested the intelligence or products. If the requestor has assigned the IR a control number, also list the control number here.

CCIR/PIR/IR: identify the supported CCIR, PIR or IR. This may be either a short text description or its control number.

Likely Collection Timeframe: ranges from "anytime" to specific windows of opportunity for collection (for example, related to anticipated time or operational phase requirements).

Source: source of intelligence collection. This may be depicted either by intelligence discipline (for example, SIGNET, ground reconnaissance) or by specific collector (for example, unmanner aerial vehicle, EA-6B, HUMINT exploitation team).

Who Needs Intelligence First: most immediate distribution recipient(s). This may be the original requestor and/or a list of units identified during COA wargaming. Specifically identify each unit by unit name, staff section or node.

Timeliness: (hours, minutes, seconds). Factor in users who need finished analysis and who needs semi-finished, single-source analysis.

Currency: (hours, minutes, seconds): Usually there is a direct proportional relationship between timeliness and currency requirements. Basic intelligence analysts, for example, may need current information for event by event analysis, but their timeliness requirements are less critical than that needed by I&W analysts or the G-3.

Periodicity of Reporting: (days, hours, minutes, seconds or as event occurs): Usually used when reporting surveillance results or tracking critical threat targets or emerging events. Nothing significant to report or negative reports are required unless otherwise directed.

General Product Type: Some examples follow:

- Structured text—usually to fill a database (e.g., order of battle database) or correlator (e.g., electronic intelligence correlator).
- Unstructured text—freeform.
- Raw digital stream—usually to fill a database or correlator.
- Analog voice.
- Digital voice.
- Video (tape or digital stream).
- Raster graphic (scanned/bitmapped photos, maps).
- Vector graphic (vector maps, some imagery products).
- Combination of formats.

Specific/Unique Product Requirements: for each general product type, identify any specific or unique product or format requirements.

Standard Channel(s): identify the primary and first alternate communication channel for standard reporting.

Alarm Channel(s): identify the primary and first alternate communication channel for time-sensitive dissemination.

Quantity: usually only used for hardcopy dissemination. Identify specific quantity for each recipient.

Deliberate Follow-up: identify if positive personal follow-up is required with any recipient subsequent to dissemination. If so, state who is responsible, with whom and when. Such follow-up is typically required when answering a CCIR.

Acknowledge Receipt Necessary? Yes or No. The communications data network may do this automatically.

APPENDIX D
INTELLIGENCE REPORTS
DISSEMINATION MATRIX FORMAT

This appendix provides a sample of an intelligence report dissemination matrix, used to ensure understanding and efficiency in dissemination of intelligence reports. It may be used as an exhibit to Tab E (Intelligence Reports) to Appendix 16 (Intelligence Operations Plan) to Annex B (Intelligence).

INTEL REPORT	ORIGIN	DISSEMINATION METHOD	VIA	COMMS PATH	MEF G-2/IOC FILTER

Appendix E
Glossary

Section I. Acronyms

AC/S . . . . assistant chief of staff
AO. . . . . area of operations

BDA . . . . battle damage assessment

C2 .command and control
C2PC. . . . . .command and control
     personal computer
CCIR. . . . . commander's critical information
     requirements
CE. . . . . command element
CI . . . . .counterintelligence
CIS . . . . communications and
     information systems
CM/DO . . . . .collection management/
     dissemination officer
COA . . . . course of action
COC . . . . combat operations center
COMSEC . . . . communications security
COP. . . . . common operational picture
CTP. . . . . .common tactical picture

DISUM . . . . daily intelligence summary
DOD . . . . Department of Defense
DS. . . . . direct support
DSN . . . . Defense Switched Network
DSNET . . . . Defense Secure Network

G-1 . . . . manpower or personnel officer
     (major subordinate commands
     and larger organizations)
G-2 . . . . . intelligence officer (major subordinate
     commands and larger organizations)
G-3 . . . . . . operations officer (major subordinate
     commands and larger organizations)
G-4 . . . . logistics officer (major subordinate
     commands and larger organizations)
G-5 . . . . plans officer (major subordinate
     commands and larger
     organizations)

G-6 . . . . communications and information
     systems officer (major
     subordinate commands and
     larger organizations)
GENSER. . . . . general service

HLZ. . . . . helicopter landing zone
HPT. . . . . .high-payoff targets
HPTR . . . . high-pay off target reporting
HQ. . . . . .headquarters
HUMINT . . . . .human intelligence

I&W . . . . .indications and warning
IAS . . . . .intelligence analysis system
ICR . . . . intelligence collection requirement
IDR . . . . intelligence dissemination requirement
IOC . . . . .intelligence operations center
IOW . . . . . . intelligence operations workstation
INTSUM. . . . . .intelligence summary
IPB . . . . intelligence preparation
     of the battlespace
IPR . . . . intelligence production requirement
IR . . . . .intelligence requirement
ISC . . . . intelligence support coordinator

J-2 . . . . intelligence directorate of a joint staff
J-6 . . . . .command, control, communications,
     and computer systems directorate
     of a joint staff
JDISS . . . . joint deployable intelligence
     support system
JIC . . . . joint intelligence center
JTF . . . . joint task force
JWICS. . . . . .Joint Worldwide Intelligence
     Communications System

LAN . . . . local area network
LTIOV . . . . . . latest time intelligence is of value

MAG. . . . . .Marine aircraft group

MAGTF . . . . Marine air-ground task force
MARDIV . . . . Marine division
MARFOR . . . . Marine Corps Forces
MAW . . . . Marine aircraft wing
MCDP . . . . . . Marine Corps doctrinal publication
MCRP . . . . . .Marine Corps reference publication
MCWP . . .Marine Corps warfighting publication
MEF . . . . Marine Expeditionary Force
MISREP . . . . mission report
MSC . . . . major subordinate command

MSE . . . . .major subordinate element

NGO . . . . .nongovernmental organization
NIPRNET . . . . Nonsecure Internet Protocol
Router Network

OIC . . . . .officer in charge
OPLAN . . . . .operation plan
OPORD . . . . .operation order

P&A . . . . production and analysis
PDA . . . . physical damage assessment
PERINTSUM . . . .periodic intelligence summary
PIR . . . . priority intelligence requirement

RFI . . . . request for information
RRFI . . . . . . response to request for information

SALUTE . . . . size, activity, location, unit,
time, and equipment
S-2 . . . . intelligence officer (units
and organizations below the major
subordinate command level)

S-3 . . . . operations officer (units
and organizations below the
major subordinate
command level)
S-4 . . . . logistics officer (units and
organizations below the
major subordinate
command level)
S-6 . . . . communications and information
systems officer (units and
organizations below the
major subordinate
command level)
SARC . . . . . surveillance and reconnaissance cell
SATCOM . . . . satellite communications
SCI . . . . sensitive compartmented
information
SCIF . . . . sensitive compartmented
information facility
SIGINT . . . . .signals intelligence
SIPRNET . . . . .SECRET Internet Protocol
Router Network
SOP . . . . .standing operating procedure
SSO . . . . .special security officer
SYSCON . . . . .systems control

TDN . . . . tactical data network
TECHCON . . . . .technical control
TSCIF . . . . .tactical sensitive compartmented
information facility

UHF . . . . .ultra high frequency

WAN . . . . wide-area network

Section II. Definitions

area of operations—An operational area defined by the joint force commander for land and naval forces. Areas of operation do not typically encompass the entire operational area of the joint force commander, but should be large enough for component commanders to accomplish their missions and protect their forces. Also called **AO**. (JP 1-02)

basic intelligence—Fundamental intelligence concerning the general situation, resources, capabili-

ties, and vulnerabilities of foreign countries or areas which may be used as reference material in the planning of operations at any level and in evaluating subsequent information relating to the same subject. (JP 1-02)

battle damage assessment—**1.** The timely and accurate estimate of damage resulting from the application of military force, either lethal or non-lethal, against a predetermined objective. Battle damage assessment can be applied to the employment of all types of weapon systems (air, ground, naval, and special forces weapon systems) throughout the range of military operations. Battle damage assessment is primarily an intelligence responsibility with required inputs and coordination from the operators. Battle damage assessment is composed of physical damage assessment, functional damage assessment, and target system assessment. (JP 1-02) **2.** In Marine Corps usage, the timely and accurate estimate of the damage resulting from the application of military force. BDA estimates physical damage to a particular target, functional damage to that target, and the capability of the entire target system to continue its operations. Also called **BDA**. (MCRP 5-12C)

battlespace—All aspects of air, surface, subsurface, land, space, and electromagnetic spectrum which encompass the area of influence and area of interest. (MCRP 5-12C)

collection—In Marine Corps usage, the gathering of intelligence data and information to satisfy the identified requirements. (MCRP 5-12C)

collection asset—A collection system, platform, or capability that is supporting, assigned, or attached to a particular commander. (JP 1-02)

collection management—**1.** In intelligence usage, the process of converting intelligence requirements into collection requirements, establishing priorities, tasking or coordinating with appropriate collection sources or agencies, monitoring results, and retasking, as required. (JP 1-02)

combatant command—A unified or specified command with a broad continuing mission under a single commander established and so designated by the President, through the Secretary of Defense and with the advice and assistance of the Chairman of the Joint Chiefs of Staff. Combatant

commands typically have geographic or functional responsibilities. (JP 1-02)

combat data—Data derived from reporting by operational units. (MCRP 5-12C)

combat information—Unevaluated data, gathered by or provided directly to the tactical commander which, due to its highly perishable nature or the criticality of the situation, cannot be processed into tactical intelligence in time to satisfy the user's tactical intelligence requirements. See also **information**. (JP 1-02)

command and control—**1.** The exercise of authority and direction by a properly designated commander over assigned and attached forces in the accomplishment of the mission. Command and control functions are performed through an arrangement of personnel, equipment, communications, facilities, and procedures employed by a commander in planning, directing, coordinating, and controlling forces and operations in the accomplishment of the mission. (JP 1-02) **2.** Also in Marine Corps usage, the means by which a commander recognizes what needs to be done and sees to it that appropriate actions are taken. Also called **C2**. (MCRP 5-12C)

commander's critical information requirements—Information regarding the enemy and friendly activities and the environment identified by the commander as critical to maintaining situational awareness, planning future activities, and facilitating timely decisionmaking. Also called **CCIR**. **NOTE**: CCIRs are normally divided into three primary subcategories: priority intelligence requirements; friendly force information requirements; and essential elements of friendly information. (MCRP 5-12C)

commander's intent—A commander's clear, concise articulation of the purpose(s) behind one or more tasks assigned to a subordinate. It is one of two parts of every mission statement which guides the exercise of initiative in the absence of instructions. (MCRP 5-12C)

commander's planning guidance—Directions and/or instructions which focus the staff's course of action development during the planning process. Also called **CPG**. (MCRP 5-12C)

component—One of the subordinate organizations that constitute a joint force. Normally a joint force is organized with a combination of Service and functional components. (JP 1-02)

coordination—The action necessary to ensure adequately integrated relationships between separate organizations located in the same area. Coordination may include such matters as fire support, emergency defense measures, area intelligence, and other situations in which coordination is considered necessary. (MCRP 5-12C)

counterintelligence—**1.** Information gathered and activities conducted to protect against espionage, other intelligence activities, sabotage, or assassinations conducted by or on behalf of foreign governments or elements thereof, foreign organizations, or foreign persons, or international terrorist activities. (JP 1-02) **2.** Within the Marine Corps, counterintelligence constitutes active and passive measures intended to deny a threat force valuable information about the friendly situation, to detect and neutralize hostile intelligence collection, and to deceive the enemy as to friendly capabilities and intentions. Also called **CI**. (MCRP 5-12C)

critical information—Specific facts about friendly intentions, capabilities, and activities vitally needed by adversaries for them to plan and act effectively so as to guarantee failure or unacceptable consequences for friendly mission accomplishment. (JP 1-02)

critical intelligence—Intelligence that is crucial and requires the immediate attention of the commander. It is required to enable the

commander to make decisions that will provide a timely and appropriate response to actions by the potential or actual enemy. It includes but is not limited to the following: a. strong indications of the imminent outbreak of hostilities of any type (warning of attack); b. aggression of any nature against a friendly country; c. indications or use of nuclear, biological, and chemical weapons (targets); and d. significant events within potential enemy countries that may lead to modification of nuclear strike plans. (JP 1-02)

critical vulnerability—An aspect of a center of gravity that if exploited will do the most significant damage to an adversary's ability to resist. A vulnerability cannot be critical unless it undermines a key strength. Also called **CV**. (MCRP 5-12C)

daily intelligence summary—A report prepared in message form at the joint force headquarters that provides higher, lateral, and subordinate headquarters with a summary of all significant intelligence produced during the previous 24-hour period. The "as of" time for information, content, and submission time for the report will be specified by the joint force commander. Also called **DISUM**. (JP 1-02)

data—Representation of facts, concepts, or instructions in a formalized manner suitable for communication, interpretation, or processing by humans or by automatic means. Any representations such as characters or analog quantities to which meaning is or might be assigned. (JP 1-02)

database—Information that is normally structured and indexed for user access and review. Databases may exist in the form of physical files (folders, documents, etc.) or formatted automated data processing system data files. (JP 1-02)

debriefing—Interviewing of an individual who has completed an intelligence or reconnaissance assignment or who has knowledge, whether through observation, participation, or otherwise, of operational or intelligence significance. (MCRP5-12C)

decision point—An event, area, or point in the battlespace where and when the friendly commander will make a critical decision. Also called **DP**. (MCRP 5-12C)

deliberate planning—A planning process for the deployment and employment of apportioned forces and resources that occurs in response to a hypothetical situation. Deliberate planners rely heavily on assumptions regarding the circumstances that will exist when the plan is executed. (JP 1-02)

descriptive intelligence—Class of intelligence which describes existing and previously existing conditions with the intent to promote situational awareness. Descriptive intelligence has two components: basic intelligence, which is general background knowledge about established and relatively constant conditions; and current intelligence, which is concerned with describing the existing situation. (MCRP 5-12C)

detachment—**1.** A part of a unit separated from its main organization for duty elsewhere. **2.** A temporary military or naval unit formed from other units or parts of units. (JP 1-02)

direct support—A mission requiring a force to support another specific force and authorizing it to answer directly to the supported force's request for assistance. Also called **DS**. (JP 1-02)

dissemination—Delivery of intelligence to users in a suitable form. (This term and its definition are proposed for inclusion in the next edition of MCRP 5-12C.)

dissemination management—Involves establishing dissemination priorities, selection of dissemination means, and monitoring the flow of intelligence throughout the command. The objective of dissemination management is to deliver the required intelligence to the appropriate user in proper form at the right time while ensuring that

individual consumers and the dissemination system are not overloaded attempting to move unneeded or irrelevant information. Dissemination management also provides for use of security controls which do not impede the timely delivery or subsequent use of intelligence while protecting intelligence sources and methods. (MCRP 5-12C)

electronic reconnaissance—The detection, location, identification, and evaluation of foreign electromagnetic radiations. (JP 1-02)

electronic warfare—Any military action involving the use of electromagnetic and directed energy to control the electromagnetic spectrum or to attack the enemy. The three major subdivisions within electronic warfare are electronic attack, electronic protection, and electronic warfare support. Also called **EW**. (JP 1-02)

essential elements of friendly information—**1.** Key questions likely to be asked by adversary officials and intelligence systems about specific friendly intentions, capabilities, and activities so they can obtain answers critical to their operational effectiveness. (JP 1-02) **2.** Specific facts about friendly intentions, capabilities, and activities needed by adversaries to plan and execute effective operations against our forces. Also called **EEFI**. (MCRP 5-12C)

fires—The effects of lethal or nonlethal weapons. (JP 1-02)

force protection—Actions taken to prevent or mitigate hostile actions against Department of Defense personnel (to include family members), resources, facilities, and critical information. These actions conserve the force's fighting potential so it can be applied at the decisive time and place and incorporate the coordinated and synchronized offensive and defensive measures to enable the effective employment of the joint force while degrading opportunities for the enemy. Force protection does not include actions to defeat the enemy or protect against accidents, weather, or disease. Also called **FP**. (JP 1-02)

force reconnaissance company—A unit whose mission is to conduct preassault and deep postassault reconnaissance operations in support of a landing force and its subordinate elements. (MCRP 5-12C)

friendly force information requirements—Information the commander needs about friendly forces in order to develop plans and make effective decisions. Depending upon the circumstances, information on unit location, composition, readiness, personnel status, and logistics status could become a friendly force information requirement. Also called **FFIR**. (MCRP 5-12C)

geographic intelligence—The process of collecting, organizing, analyzing, synthesizing, disseminating, and using all-source geospatial and other intelligence information with regard to the military aspects of the terrain in support of MAGTF operations. GEOINT can include cross-country movement studies, line of sight analysis, natural and manmade obstacles, and various terrain studies (e.g., road, railroad, airfield, bridges, ports, helicopter landing zones). Also called **GEOINT**. (This term and its definition are proposed for inclusion in the next edition of MCRP 5-12C.)

global sourcing—A process of force provision or augmentation whereby resources may be drawn from any location/command worldwide. (MCRP 5-12C)

helicopter landing zone—A specified ground area for landing assault helicopters to embark or disembark troops and/or cargo. A landing zone may contain one or more landing sites. Also called **HLZ**. (JP 1-02)

high-payoff target—A target whose loss to the enemy will significantly contribute to the success of the friendly course of action. High-payoff targets are those high-value targets that must be acquired and successfully attacked for the success of the friendly commander's mission. Also called **HPT**. See also **high-value target**. (JP 1-02)

high-value target—A target the enemy commander requires for the successful completion of the mission. The loss of high-value targets would be expected to seriously degrade important enemy functions throughout the friendly commander's area of interest. Also called **HVT**. See also **high-payoff target**. (JP 1-02)

human intelligence—1. A category of intelligence derived from information collected and provided by human sources. (JP 1-02) 2. In Marine Corps usage, human intelligence operations cover a wide range of activities encompassing reconnaissance patrols, aircrew reports and debriefs, debriefing of refugees, interrogations of prisoners of war, and the conduct of counterintelligence force protection source operations. Also called **HUMINT**. (MCRP 5-12C)

hydrography—The science which deals with the measurements and description of the physical features of the oceans, seas, lakes, rivers, and their adjoining coastal areas, with particular reference to their use for navigational purposes. (JP 1-02)

imagery intelligence—Intelligence derived from the exploitation of collection by visual photography, infrared sensors, lasers, electro-optics, and radar sensors such as synthetic aperture radar wherein images of objects are reproduced optically or electronically on film, electronic display devices, or other media. Also called **IMINT**. (JP 1-02)

indications and warning—Those intelligence activities intended to detect and report time-sensitive intelligence information on foreign developments that could involve a threat to the US or allied and/or coalition military, political, or economic interests or to US citizens abroad. It includes forewarning of enemy actions or intentions; the imminence of hostilities; insurgency; nuclear/non-nuclear attack on the US, its overseas forces, or allied and/or coalition nations; hostile reactions to US reconnaissance activities; terrorists' attacks; and other similar events. Also called **I&W**. See **information**; **intelligence**. (JP 1-02)

information—**1.** Facts, data, or instructions in any medium or form. **2.** The meaning that a human assigns to data by means of the known conventions used in their representation. (JP 1-02)

integration—A stage in the intelligence cycle in which a pattern is formed through the selection and combination of evaluated information. (This term and its definition are proposed for inclusion in the next edition of MCRP 5-12C.)

intelligence—**1.** The product resulting from the collection, processing, integration, analysis, evaluation, and interpretation of available information concerning foreign countries or areas. **2.** Information and knowledge about an adversary obtained through observation, investigation, analysis, or understanding. (JP 1-02) 3. Also, in Marine Corps usage, intelligence is knowledge about the enemy or the surrounding environment needed to support decisionmaking. This knowledge is the result of the collection, processing, exploitation, evaluation, integration, analysis, and interpretation of available information about the battlespace and threat. (MCRP 5-12C)

intelligence annex—A supporting document of an operation plan or order that provides detailed information on the enemy situation, assignment of intelligence tasks, and intelligence administrative procedures. (JP 1-02)

intelligence cycle—The process by which information is converted into intelligence and made available to users. (JP 1-02)

intelligence data—Data derived from assets primarily dedicated to intelligence collection such as imagery systems, electronic intercept equipment, human intelligence sources, etc. (MCRP 5-12C)

intelligence discipline—A well defined area of intelligence collection, processing, exploitation, and reporting using a specific category of technical or human resources. There are seven major disciplines: human intelligence, imagery intelligence, measurement and signature intelligence, signals intelligence (communications intelligence, electronic intelligence, and foreign instrumentation signals intelligence), open-source intelligence, technical intelligence, and counterintelligence. (JP 1-02)

intelligence estimate—The appraisal, expressed in writing or orally, of available intelligence relating to a specific situation or condition with a view to determining the courses of action open to the enemy or potential enemy and the order of probability of their adoption. (JP 1-02)

intelligence operations—The variety of intelligence tasks that are carried out by various intelligence organizations and activities. Predominantly, it refers to either intelligence collection or intelligence production activities. When used in the context of intelligence collection activities, intelligence operations refer to collection, processing, exploitation, and reporting of information. When used in the context of intelligence production activities, it refers to collation, integration, interpretation, and analysis, leading to the dissemination of a finished product. (JP 1-02)

intelligence preparation of the battlespace—**1.** An analytical methodology employed to reduce uncertainties concerning the enemy, environment, and terrain for all types of operations. Intelligence preparation of the battlespace builds an extensive database for each potential area in which a unit may be required to operate. The database is then analyzed in detail to determine the impact of the enemy, environment, and terrain on operations and presents it in graphic form. Intelligence preparation of the battlespace is a continuing process. (JP 1-02) **2.** In Marine Corps usage, the systematic, continuous process of analyzing the threat and environment in a specific geographic area. Also called **IPB**. (MCRP 5-12C)

intelligence report—A specific report of information, usually on a single item, made at any level of command in tactical operations and disseminated as rapidly as possible in keeping with the timeliness of the information. Also called **INTREP**. (JP 1-02)

intelligence requirement—**1.** Any subject, general or specific, upon which there is a need for the collection of information, or the production of intelligence. **2.** A requirement for intelligence to fill a gap in the command's knowledge or understanding of the battlespace or threat forces. (JP 1-02) **3.** In Marine Corps usage, questions about the enemy and the environment, the answers to which a commander requires to make sound decisions. Also called **IR**. (MCRP 5-12C)

joint deployable intelligence support system—A transportable workstation and communications suite that electronically extends a joint intelligence center to a joint task force or other tactical user. Also called **JDISS**. (JP 1-02)

joint force—A general term applied to a force composed of significant elements, assigned or attached, of two or more Military Departments, operating under a single joint force commander. (JP 1-02)

joint intelligence center—The intelligence center of the combatant command headquarters. The joint intelligence center is responsible for providing and producing the intelligence required to support the combatant commander and staff, components, subordinate joint forces and elements, and the national intelligence community. Also called **JIC**. (JP 1-02)

joint intelligence support element—A subordinate joint force forms a joint intelligence support element as the focus for intelligence support for

joint operations, providing the joint force commander, joint staff, and components with the complete air, space, ground, and maritime adversary situation. Also called **JISE**. (JP 1-02)

joint operations—A general term to describe military actions conducted by joint forces or by Service forces in relationships (e.g., support, coordinating authority), which, of themselves, do not create joint forces. (JP 1-02)

joint task force—A joint force that is constituted and so designated by the Secretary of Defense, a combatant commander, a subunified commander, or an existing joint task force commander. Also called **JTF**. (JP 1-02)

Joint Worldwide Intelligence Communications System—The sensitive, compartmented information portion of the Defense Information Systems Network. It incorporates advanced networking technologies that permit point-to-point or multipoint information exchange involving voice, text, graphics, data, and video teleconferencing. Also called **JWICS**. (JP 1-02)

Marine Corps Planning Process—A six-step methodology which helps organize the thought processes of the commander and staff throughout the planning and execution of military operations. It focuses on the threat and is based on the Marine Corps philosophy of maneuver warfare. It capitalizes on the principle of unity of command and supports the establishment and maintenance of tempo. The six steps consist of mission analysis, course of action development, course of action analysis, comparison/decision, orders development, and transition. Also called **MCPP**. **NOTE**: Tenets of the MCPP include top down planning, single battle concept, and integrated planning. (MCRP 5-12C)

military operations other than war—Operations that encompass the use of military capabilities across the range of military operations short of war. These military actions can be applied to complement any combination of the other instruments of national power and occur before, during, and after war. Also called **MOOTW**. (JP 1-02)

multinational operations—A collective term to describe military actions conducted by forces of two or more nations, usually undertaken within the structure of a coalition or alliance. (JP 1-02)

national intelligence support team—A nationally sourced team composed of intelligence and communications experts from either Defense Intelligence Agency, Central Intelligence Agency, National Security Agency, or any combination of these agencies. Also called **NIST**. (JP 1-02)

near real time—Pertaining to the timeliness of data or information which has been delayed by the time required for electronic communication and automatic data processing. This implies that there are no significant delays. Also called **NRT**. (JP 1-02)

noncombatant evacuation operations—Operations directed by the Department of State, the Department of Defense, or other appropriate authority whereby noncombatants are evacuated from foreign countries when their lives are endangered by war, civil unrest, or natural disaster to safe havens or the United States. Also called **NEO**. (JP 1-02)

operational control—Command authority that may be exercised by commanders at any echelon at or below the level of combatant command. Operational control is inherent in combatant command (command authority) and may be delegated within the command. When forces are transferred between combatant commands, the command relationship the gaining commander will exercise (and the losing commander will relinquish) over these forces must be specified by the Secretary of Defense. Operational control is the authority to perform those functions of command over subordinate forces involving organizing and employing commands and forces, assigning tasks, designating objectives, and giving authoritative direction necessary to accomplish the mission. Operational control includes authoritative direction over all aspects of military operations and joint training necessary to accomplish missions assigned to the command. Operational control should be exercised through the commanders of subordinate organizations. Normally this authority is exercised through joint force commanders and Service and/or functional component commanders. Operational control normally provides full authority to organize commands and forces and to employ those forces as the commander in operational control considers necessary to accomplish assigned missions; it does not, in and of itself, include authoritative direction for logistics or matters of administration, discipline, internal organization, or unit training. Also called **OPCON**. (JP 1-02)

operations control and analysis center—Main node for the command and control of radio battalion signals intelligence operations and the overall coordination of MAGTF signals intelligence operations. Processes, analyzes, produces, and disseminates signals intelligence-derived information and directs the ground-based electronic warfare activities of the radio battalion. Also called **OCAC**. (MCRP 5-12C)

order of battle—The identification, strength, command structure, and disposition of the personnel, units, and equipment of any military force. Also called **OOB**. (JP 1-02)

priority intelligence requirements—**1.** Those intelligence requirements for which a commander has an anticipated and stated priority in his task of planning and decisionmaking. (JP 1-02) **2.** In Marine Corps usage, an intelligence requirement associated with a decision that will critically affect the overall success of the command's mission. Also called **PIR**. (MCRP 5-12C)

production—Conversion of processed information into intelligence through the integration, analysis, evaluation, and interpretation of all source data and the preparation of intelligence products in support of known or anticipated user requirements. (Term and definition proposed for next edition of MCRP 5-12C.)

production management—Encompasses determining the scope, content, and format of each intelligence product, developing a plan and schedule for the development of each product, assigning priorities among the various production requirements, allocating processing, exploitation, and production resources, and integrating production efforts with intelligence collection and dissemination. (MCRP 5-12C)

reach back—The ability to exploit resources, capabilities, expertise, etc., not physically located in the theater or a joint operations area, when established. (MCRP 5-12C)

reactive target—The method used for targeting targets of opportunity. It is used when time and situation do not allow for targeting; i.e., during deliberate targeting, during an attack, when defending against an attack, or upon discovery of the location of a target such as a radio jammer, tank, or antiaircraft weapon. (MCRP 5-12C)

SECRET Internet Protocol Router Network—Worldwide SECRET level packet switch network that uses high-speed internet protocol routers and high-capacity Defense Information Systems Network circuitry. Also called **SIPRNET**. (JP 1-02)

sensitive compartmented information—All information and materials bearing special community controls indicating restricted handling within present and future community intelligence collection programs and their end products for which community systems of compartmentation have been or will be formally established. (These controls are ever and above the provisions of DOD 5200.1R, *Information Security Program Regulation*.) Also called **SCI**. (JP 1-02)

sensitive compartmented information facility—An accredited area, room, group of rooms, or installation where sensitive compartmented information (SCI) may be stored, used, discussed, and/or electroncially

processed. Sensitive compartmented information facility (SCIF) procedural and physical measures prevent the free access of persons unless they have been formally indoctrinated for the particular SCI authorized for use or storage within the SCIF. Also called **SCIF**. (JP 1-02)

sensor data—Data derived from sensors whose primary mission is surveillance or target acquisition, such as air surveillance radars, counterbattery radars, and remote ground sensors. (MCRP 5-12C)

signals intelligence—**1.** A category of intelligence information comprising either individually or in combination all communications intelligence, electronic intelligence, and foreign instrumentation signals, however transmitted. **2.** Intelligence derived from communications, electronic, and foreign instrumentation signals. Also called **SIGINT**. (JP 1-02)

situational awareness—Knowledge and understanding of the current situation which promotes timely, relevant and accurate assessment of friendly, enemy, and other operations within the battlespace in order to facilitate decisionmaking. An informational perspective and skill that foster an ability to determine quickly the context and relevance of events that are unfolding. (MCRP 5-12C)

surveillance and reconnaissance cell—Primary element responsible for the supervision of MAGTF intelligence collection operations. Directs, coordinates, and monitors intelligence collection operations conducted by organic, attached, and direct support collection assets. Also called **SARC**. (MCRP 5-12C)

tactical intelligence—**1.** Intelligence that is required for planning and conducting tactical operations. (JP 1-02) **2.** In Marine Corps usage, tactical intelligence is concerned primarily with the location, capabilities, and possible intentions of enemy units on the battlefield and with the tactical aspects of terrain and weather within the battlespace. Also called **TACINTEL**. (MCRP 5-12C)

target—**1.** An area, complex, installation, force, equipment, capability, function, or behavior identified for possible action to support the commander's objectives, guidance, and intent. Targets fall into two general categories: planned and immediate. **2.** In intelligence usage, a country, area, installation, agency, or person against which intelligence operations are directed. **3.** An area designated and numbered for future firing. **4.** In gunfire support usage, an impact burst that hits the target. Also called **TGT**. (JP 1-02)

target intelligence—Intelligence that portrays and locates the components of a target or target complex and indicates its vulnerability and relative importance. See also **target**. (JP 1-02)

track management—Defined set of procedures whereby the commander ensures accurate friendly and enemy unit and/or platform locations, and a dissemination procedure for filtering, combining, and passing that information to higher, adjacent, and subordinate commanders. (JP 1-02)

warfighting functions—The six mutually supporting military activities integrated in the conduct of all military operations are: **1. command and control**—The means by which a commander recognizes what needs to be done and sees to it that appropriate actions are taken. **2. maneuver**—The movement of forces for the purpose of gaining an advantage over the enemy. **3. fires**—Those means used to delay, disrupt, degrade, or destroy enemy capabilities, forces, or facilities as well as affect the enemy's will to fight. **4. intelligence**—Knowledge about the enemy or the surrounding environment needed to support decisionmaking. **5. logistics**—All activities required to move and sustain military forces. **6. force protection**—Actions or efforts used to safeguard own centers of gravity while protecting, concealing, reducing, or eliminating friendly critical vulnerabilities. Also called **WF**. (MCRP 5-12C)

APPENDIX F
REFERENCES

Joint Publications (JPs)

1-02	Department of Defense Dictionary of Military and Associated Terms
2-0	Doctrine for Intelligence Support to Joint Operations
2-01	Joint Intelligence Support to Military Operations
2-02	National Intelligence Support to Joint Operations
2-03	Joint Tactics, Techniques, and Procedures for Geospatial Information and Services Support to Joint Operations

Marine Corps Doctrinal Publications (MCDPs)

1	Warfighting
1-0	Marine Corps Operations
1-1	Strategy
1-2	Campaigning
1-3	Tactics
2	Intelligence
3	Expeditionary Operations
4	Logistics
5	Planning
6	Command and Control

Marine Corps Warfighting Publications (MCWPs)

2-1	Intelligence Operations
2-12	MAGTF Intelligence Production and Analysis
2-12.1	Geographic Intelligence
2-14	Counterintelligence
2-15.1	Remote Sensor Operations
2-15.2	Signals Intelligence
2-15.4	Imagery Intelligence
3-2	Aviation Operations

3-40.2	Information Management
3-40.3	Communications and Information Systems
5-1	Marine Corps Planning Process

Marine Corps Reference Publications (MCRPs)

2-1D	Multi-Service Procedures for Requesting Reconnaissance Information in Joint Environment (RECCE-J)
2-1E	Multi-Service Procedures for the Joint Surveillance Target Attack Radar System (J-STARS)
2-12A	Intelligence Preparation of the Battlespace
2-15.3B	Reconnaissance Reports Guide
5-12A	Operational Terms and Graphics
5-12C	Marine Corps Supplement to the Department of Defense Dictionary of Military and Associated Terms
5-12D	Organization of Marine Corps Forces